RIVER CAFE
POCKET BOOKS
PASTA
& RAVIOLI

RIVER CAFE
POCKET BOOKS
PASTA
& RAVIOLI

ROSE GRAY AND RUTH ROGERS

Introduction

Chapter one
Raw sauces 1-12

Chapter two
Cheese sauces 13-22

Chapter three
Vegetarian sauces 23-49

Chapter four
Fish sauces 50-71

Chapter five
Meat sauces 72-88

Chapter six
Stuffed pasta 89-97

Chapter seven
Gnocchi & gnudi 98-105

Index

Introduction

Pasta is the most comforting of all Italian food. With its variety of sauces it is cooked at least once a day by almost every cook in every region of Italy. It's easy to prepare and good for you as well.

There are three basic kinds of pasta. The best known is the dried durum wheat and water pasta such as spaghetti and penne. The second are the dried pastas made with eggs and plain flour cut into different width ribbons to make tagliatelle and pappardelle. These are an excellent substitute for the third, fresh pasta – a rich combination of whole eggs, yolks and the fine 'Tipo 00' flour – fun to make but time-consuming.

When cooking pasta always use a saucepan large enough to hold 5 litres of water for every 500 grams of pasta. Add salt when the water boils, and have a large colander ready in the sink so that the pasta can be drained immediately. Cooking time will depend on the kind of pasta you're using – durum wheat takes up to fifteen minutes, dried egg pasta takes up to eight minutes while fresh pasta takes just a few minutes. Pasta is ready when it is 'al dente' – cooked, but still firm to bite.

When combining the sauce with the pasta, it is vital to toss and toss again, either in the hot pan the sauce was cooked in or the one the pasta was cooked in. Most importantly keep the pasta hot and slippery and serve immediately on heated plates.

All recipes serve four unless otherwise stated. All herbs are fresh unless otherwise stated. All eggs are large, free-range, organic unless otherwise stated. Wash all fresh herbs, fruits and vegetables in cold water before use.

CHAPTER ONE RAW SAUCES

1 Penne with capers, tomatoes and ricotta salata
2 Orecchiette with tomatoes and fresh ricotta
3 Bucatini with dried oregano • 4 Spaghetti with
artichoke and parsley pesto • 5 Spaghetti with plum
tomatoes, capers and olives • 6 Taglierini with fresh
porcini • 7 Spaghetti with cherry tomatoes and two
vinegars • 8 Tagliatelle with fresh hazelnuts
9 Taglierini with white truffles • 10 Tagliatelle with
fresh walnuts • 11 Tagliatelle with green beans
12 Taglierini with raw broad beans

1 Penne with capers, tomatoes and ricotta salata

350g Penne • 3 tbs Salted capers, rinsed of all their salt • 1kg Red and yellow cherry tomatoes • 6 Sundried tomatoes • 1 tbs Red wine vinegar • 1 Dried red chilli, crumbled • 2 Garlic cloves, peeled and squashed in 1 tbs sea salt • 2 tbs Roughly torn basil leaves • 100g Ricotta salata, freshly grated • Extra virgin olive oil

Add the vinegar to the capers and leave them for 5 minutes. Cut the tomatoes in half and squeeze out the juice and seeds, using a sieve set over a bowl to collect the juices.

Pulse-chop the sundried tomatoes with the capers and vinegar and add 3 tbs of olive oil, drop by drop, to make a rough purée. Season with the chilli.

Mix the garlic with the tomato juice and add to the purée. Stir to combine. Place in a large serving bowl and mix with half the tomatoes and half the basil.

Cook the penne in boiling salted water until al dente, then drain, keeping back 2 tbs of the pasta water. Add the penne and the water to the tomato sauce along with the remaining tomatoes and basil. Toss together and serve with the ricotta.

Ricotta salata is a hard, salted sheep's milk cheese that is used instead of Parmesan to grate over pasta in the south of Italy.

2   Orecchiette with tomatoes and fresh ricotta

*350g Orecchiette • 500g Cherry tomatoes, or ripe
small juicy tomatoes • 200g Fresh ricotta • 1 Garlic
clove, peeled and chopped • 2 tbs Roughly torn basil
leaves • 50g Parmesan, freshly grated • Extra virgin
olive oil*

Cut the tomatoes in half, squeeze out the seeds over
a sieve to collect the juice. Combine the tomatoes
and their juice with the garlic. Season, add 2 tbs of
olive oil and toss to combine. Leave to marinate for at
least 30 minutes.

Put the fresh ricotta in a bowl, lightly season and mix
with a fork.

Cook the orecchiette in boiling salted water until al
dente, then drain.

Gently heat the tomato mixture, add the orecchiette
and basil and stir to combine. Finally, fold in the
ricotta. Serve with a drizzle of olive oil and the
Parmesan.

*Ricotta is a mild fresh cheese made by re-heating
the whey of the milk which naturally separates during
the cheese process. The light, creamy curds are
traditionally shaped in baskets. Ricotta is made from
cow's, sheep's goat and buffalo milk depending on
the region and tradition. Fresh ricotta does not keep for
more than 3-4 days.*

3 Bucatini with dried oregano

*340g Bucatini • 4 tbs Fresh oregano, roughly chopped
• 2 tbs Dried oregano • 1kg Red and yellow cherry
tomatoes, halved and squeezed to remove juice and
seeds • Extra virgin olive oil*

Mix the fresh and dried oregano together.

Season the tomatoes generously and stir in 3 tbs of
olive oil.

Cook the bucatini in boiling salted water until al
dente, then drain and return to the saucepan. Add
1 tbs of olive oil and the oregano mixture, then toss
to coat each strand. Serve with the marinated
tomatoes on top.

*It is very important with this recipe to use ripe, soft
cherry tomatoes and the best-quality extra virgin
olive oil.*

4 Spaghetti with artichoke and parsley pesto

*350g Spaghetti • 3 Globe artichokes • 4 tbs
Flat-leaf parsley (keep the stalks) • 3 Garlic cloves,
peeled and halved • 50g Pine nuts • 125g Parmesan,
freshly grated, plus extra for serving • 100ml Milk •
50g Unsalted butter • Extra virgin olive oil*

To prepare the artichokes, cut the stalks 5cm from
the heads and pull away the tough outer leaves.

Cut off the tips of the remaining leaves and peel the fibres from the stalks. Cut each heart in half and remove the choke, if any. Put the pieces into water with the parsley stalks as you go, to prevent the artichokes turning brown.

To make the pesto, use a food processor with a sharp blade. Drain the artichokes and pat dry. Place in the food processor with the garlic, pine nuts, parsley leaves and Parmesan. Add the milk and blend to a rough pulp, then slowly add 100ml olive oil to form a thick cream. Season.

Cook the spaghetti in boiling salted water until al dente. Drain, reserving 2 tbs of the cooking water. Return to the pan with the cooking water. Add the pesto sauce and the butter. Stir to combine, then serve with the extra Parmesan.

5 Spaghetti with plum tomatoes, capers and olives

350g Spaghetti • 4 Plum tomatoes, halved, squeezed and quartered • 2 tbs Salted capers, rinsed of all their salt • 3 tbs Black olives, stoned • 2 Garlic cloves, peeled and squashed in 1 tbs sea salt • 2 Dried red chillies, crumbled • 3 tbs Roughly chopped rocket • Extra virgin olive oil

Combine the tomatoes with the garlic, capers, olives and dried chillies. Season with black pepper. Stir in 3 tbs of olive oil.

Cook the spaghetti in boiling salted water until al dente, then drain. Return the pasta to the saucepan and, over a low heat, add the tomato mixture and rocket. Toss to combine and serve drizzled with olive oil.

6 Taglierini with fresh porcini

350g Taglierini • 1kg Fresh porcini mushrooms, wiped clean • 50g Unsalted butter • 2 Garlic cloves, peeled and finely chopped • 3 tbs Finely chopped flat-leaf parsley • 150ml Double cream • 60g Parmesan, freshly grated • Extra virgin olive oil

Separate the stalks and caps of the porcini. Trim the stalks and roughly chop. Finely slice the caps, keeping them separate from the stalks.

Melt the butter with 2 tbs of olive oil in a thick-bottomed pan, add the porcini stalks, garlic and parsley and cook gently for 4 minutes, until soft but not brown. Season.

Cook the taglierini in boiling salted water until al dente. Drain, keeping 3 tbs of the pasta water. Add the taglierini to the stalk mixture, then stir in the cream and the retained pasta water. Heat through.

Serve with the sliced porcini caps scattered over each plate. Sprinkle with sea salt and the Parmesan, and drizzle with olive oil.

7 Spaghetti with cherry tomatoes and two vinegars

350g Spaghetti • 600g Cherry tomatoes, halved and squeezed to remove juice and seeds • 2 tbs Red wine vinegar • 1 tbs Traditional balsamic vinegar • 3 tbs Roughly torn basil leaves • Extra virgin olive oil

In a bowl, combine 6 tbs of olive oil with the vinegars and season. Add the tomato halves, pressing them down to absorb the flavours of the vinegar and oil. Add half the basil, stir, then cover and leave to marinate for an hour or more. Do not refrigerate.

Cook the spaghetti in boiling salted water until al dente. Drain and return to the pan. Add the tomato mixture over a high heat, tossing to combine and coat the pasta. Add the remaining basil and drizzle with olive oil to serve.

Spaghetti with cherry tomatoes and two vinegars (Recipe 7)

8 Tagliatelle with fresh hazelnuts

350g Dried egg tagliatelle • 250g Fresh hazelnuts (shelled weight) • 2 Garlic cloves, peeled • 300ml Double cream • 50ml Brandy • 2 tsp Cocoa powder, with 100% cocoa solids • 1/3 Nutmeg, freshly grated • 100g Parmesan, freshly grated, plus extra for serving • 1 Dried red chilli, crumbled • Extra virgin olive oil

Preheat the oven to 200°C/Gas Mark 6.

Place the hazelnuts on a baking tray and roast for 10 minutes, or until the skins become loose. Place on a tea towel, fold it over the hot nuts and rub vigorously to remove the skins. Shake the nuts in a coarse sieve to remove any remaining skin. Allow to cool.

Place the nuts and garlic in a food processor and briefly pulse-chop. Add the cream, brandy and 100ml of olive oil. Blend until a creamy texture, then stir in the cocoa powder, nutmeg and Parmesan. Season with salt, pepper and the chilli.

Cook the tagliatelle in boiling salted water until al dente. Drain, keeping back 3 tbs of the pasta water. Mix the sauce with the tagliatelle, adding the pasta water if too thick. Serve with the extra Parmesan and olive oil drizzled over.

Hazelnuts grow in abundance throughout Italy. Although usually associated with cakes, nougat and the chocolate known as Gianduia, they are also used in sauces for meat and fish as well as pasta.

9 Taglierini with white truffles

*350g Dried egg taglierini • 70-80g White truffles •
150g Unsalted butter, softened • ¼ tsp Freshly
grated nutmeg*

Carefully clean the truffles of dirt, using a toothbrush
under a slow-dripping tap. Dry on kitchen paper.

Cook the taglierini in boiling salted water until al
dente. Drain, keeping back 2 tbs of the pasta water.

Gently melt the butter, add the nutmeg and a few
shavings of truffle. Mix in the 2 tbs of pasta water. Stir
in the taglierini and toss to coat each strand. Serve on
warm plates with a generous amount of truffle shaved
over each plate.

10 Tagliatelle with fresh walnuts

350g Dried egg tagliatelle • 1.5kg Wet walnuts, shelled and bitter skins removed, plus 300g to serve • Breadcrumbs from ½ ciabatta loaf, crusts removed • 100ml Milk • 2 Garlic cloves, peeled • 2 tbs Roughly chopped flat-leaf parsley • 80g Parmesan, freshly grated, plus extra for serving • 75g Unsalted butter • Extra virgin olive oil

Soak the breadcrumbs in the milk. Place the walnuts and garlic in a food processor and pulse-chop. Add the parsley and some salt and pulse briefly. Gently squeeze the milk from the breadcrumbs, keeping the milk. Add the breadcrumbs to the nuts and pulse until a rough paste. Slowly add 120ml olive oil, blending all the time, and then finally add the Parmesan. If the sauce is too stiff, stir in the reserved milk.

Cook the tagliatelle in boiling salted water until al dente. Drain, reserving 2 tbs of the pasta water. Return the pasta to the saucepan, add the butter and the pasta water, then toss. Add the sauce and stir well to coat the tagliatelle. Serve with the extra Parmesan and a few pieces of uncrushed walnut.

11 Tagliatelle with green beans

350g Dried egg tagliatelle • 250g Fine green beans, topped and tailed • 500g Plum tomatoes, halved, squeezed and roughly chopped • 150ml Double cream • 2 Garlic cloves, peeled and cut in half • 3 tbs

Basil leaves • 50g Parmesan, freshly grated

Cook the green beans in boiling salted water until tender, then drain. Season the tomatoes generously with salt and pepper.

Bring the cream to the boil in a thick-bottomed saucepan with the garlic, then simmer gently for 5 minutes. Remove the garlic pieces. Add the tomatoes, green beans and basil to the cream.

Cook the tagliatelle in boiling salted water until al dente. Drain, then add to the tomatoes and beans. Serve with the Parmesan.

12 Taglierini with raw broad beans

350g Dried egg taglierini • 1.5kg Fresh broad beans (podded weight, 400g) • 150g Pecorino, freshly grated • 2 Garlic cloves, peeled • 3 tbs Basil leaves • Juice of 1 lemon • Extra virgin olive oil

Place two-thirds of the broad beans in a food processor with the garlic, basil and 1 tsp of sea salt and pulse-chop to a coarse pulp. Remove to a large bowl and slowly stir in 120ml olive oil. Stir in the remaining whole beans and two-thirds of the pecorino. Finally, add the lemon juice and mix.

Cook the taglierini in boiling salted water until al dente. Drain, reserving 3 tbs of the pasta water. Return the taglierini and water to the saucepan, add the sauce and, over the heat, toss for 2 minutes to coat the pasta. Serve with the remaining pecorino.

Taglierini with raw broad beans (Recipe 12)

CHAPTER TWO
CHEESE SAUCES

13 Penne with zucchini and ricotta • 14 Rigatoni
with fontina • 15 Spaghetti with lemon
16 Spaghetti with pecorino • 17 Conchiglie
with ricotta and rocket • 18 Tagliatelle with
mascarpone and fried breadcrumbs • 19 Tagliatelle
with crème fraîche and rocket • 20 Tagliatelle
with lemon, cream and parsley • 21 Tagliatelle
with gorgonzola • 22 Tagliatelle with asparagus

13 Penne with zucchini and ricotta

350g Penne • 1kg Small zucchini, trimmed of stalks and tips • 350g Ricotta • 4 Garlic cloves, peeled and finely sliced • 3 tbs Roughly chopped basil • 100g Parmesan, freshly grated • Extra virgin olive oil

Cook the zucchini whole in boiling salted water for 2 minutes, then drain. Slice at an angle, 1cm thick.

Heat 2 tbs of olive oil in a thick-bottomed pan and fry the garlic in it until soft and lightly coloured. Add the zucchini and toss over a low heat to combine the flavours. Season and add the basil.

Cook the penne in boiling salted water until al dente, then drain. Add to the zucchini and stir to combine. Crumble over the ricotta. Serve with the Parmesan.

14 Rigatoni with fontina

350g Rigatoni (12-minute cooking time) • ½ Savoy cabbage, discard tough leaves, cut into eighths • 200g Fontina, cut into 1cm pieces • 150g Unsalted butter • 2 Garlic cloves, peeled and finely sliced • 6 Anchovy fillets • 2 Dried red chillies, crumbled • ⅓ Nutmeg, grated • 250g Potatoes, peeled and sliced 5mm thick • 100g Parmesan, freshly grated

Cook the cabbage in boiling salted water until tender. Drain, then chop.

Melt half the butter in a thick-bottomed pan, add the garlic and fry until soft. Add the anchovies and stir to melt over a low heat. Add the chilli, nutmeg and cabbage. Mix to combine the flavours.

Cook the rigatoni in boiling salted water until al dente, adding the potatoes after 6 minutes. Drain, reserving 3 tbs of the water.

Add the pasta and potatoes to the cabbage, then stir in the remaining butter. Add the fontina and the reserved pasta water. Cover for 1 minute to allow the cheese to melt into the sauce. Serve with the Parmesan.

15 Spaghetti with lemon

340g Spaghetti • Zest and juice of 2 lemons • 200g Parmesan, freshly grated, plus extra for serving • 4 tbs Roughly chopped basil • Extra virgin olive oil

Slowly stir the lemon juice and zest into the Parmesan until you have a thick sauce, then add enough olive oil to make a thick, creamy consistency. Season and taste, adding more oil if the sauce is too tart.

Cook the spaghetti in boiling salted water until al dente. Drain, keeping back 2 tbs of the cooking water. Return to the pan. Stir in the sauce, making sure each strand is coated. Add the cooking water to loosen the mixture. Add the basil and serve with the extra Parmesan.

16 Spaghetti with pecorino

340g Spaghetti • 100g Pecorino Romano, grated • 150g Unsalted butter • ½ tbs Coarsely ground black pepper

Cook the spaghetti in boiling salted water until al dente. Drain, reserving 4 tbs of the water. Put this water and the butter into a hot saucepan with the black pepper and stir to combine.

Remove from the heat and stir in half the pecorino. Add the spaghetti and toss to coat thoroughly. Check for seasoning. Serve with the remaining pecorino.

17 Conchiglie with ricotta and rocket

350g Conchiglie • 200g Ricotta, lightly beaten with a fork • 500g Rocket, roughly chopped • 3 Garlic cloves, peeled and sliced • 3 tbs Torn basil leaves • 3 Fresh red chillies, cut in half lengthways, de-seeded and chopped • 150g Parmesan, freshly grated • Extra virgin olive oil

Heat 2 tbs of olive oil in a small, thick-bottomed pan. Add the garlic and fry until it begins to colour. Add the basil and half the rocket. Cover, reduce the heat and cook for 2-3 minutes just to wilt the rocket.

Put this mixture, including any liquid, into a food processor and pulse-chop. Add half the remaining rocket, the chillies, seasoning and 2 tbs of olive oil. Blend briefly to combine.

Cook the conchiglie in boiling salted water until al dente, then drain, keeping back a little of the pasta water. Add the rocket mixture to the pasta. Lightly stir in the ricotta and the remaining uncooked rocket. Serve with a drizzle of olive oil and the Parmesan.

Conchiglie with ricotta and rocket (Recipe 17)

18 Tagliatelle with mascarpone and fried breadcrumbs

340g Dried egg tagliatelle • 350g Mascarpone cheese • ½ Ciabatta loaf, bottom crust removed, made into crumbs • 3 Egg yolks • 6 Garlic cloves, 1 squashed in 1 tbs sea salt, 5 peeled but left whole • 80g Parmesan, freshly grated • 2 tbs Finely chopped thyme • 2 tbs Finely chopped marjoram • Extra virgin olive oil

Stir the egg yolks into the mascarpone, then add 100ml olive oil, drop by drop as you would for mayonnaise. Stir in the squashed garlic and the Parmesan.

To fry the breadcrumbs, heat 150ml olive oil in a small, thick-bottomed saucepan and add the whole garlic cloves. Cook until the cloves are a deep gold, then remove them. Add the breadcrumbs to the hot, flavoured oil and cook until they become golden. Add the herbs and then immediately drain the breadcrumb mixture. Lay out the breadcrumbs on kitchen paper to drain off excess oil.

Cook the tagliatelle in boiling salted water until al dente, then drain, keeping back a little of the pasta water. Add to the mascarpone and toss to combine, adding some of the cooking water to loosen the sauce. Serve covered with the breadcrumbs.

19 Tagliatelle with crème fraîche and rocket

*340g Dried egg tagliatelle • 250ml Crème fraîche •
150g Rocket, roughly chopped • Zest and juice of
2 lemons • 100g Parmesan, freshly grated*

Put the crème fraîche in a bowl and add the lemon
juice and zest. Season.

Cook the tagliatelle in boiling salted water until al
dente, then drain and return to the pan. Add the
rocket and stir, then pour over the crème fraîche. Toss
to combine. Stir briefly over the heat and serve with
the Parmesan.

20 Tagliatelle with lemon, cream

340g Dried egg tagliatelle • Zest and juice of 3 lemons • 300ml Double cream • 3 tbs Roughly chopped flat-leaf parsley • 110g Unsalted butter, softened • 100g Parmesan, freshly grated

Gently heat the cream in a small, thick-bottomed saucepan. When warm, add the butter and the lemon zest and juice. Stir to combine, then remove from the heat.

Cook the tagliatelle in boiling salted water until al dente, then drain. Stir into the warm cream and season. Add half the parsley and toss together.

Serve with the remainder of the parsley sprinkled over, and the Parmesan.

21 Tagliatelle with gorgonzola

350g Dried egg tagliatelle • 220g Gorgonzola, naturale, broken up into 2cm pieces • 250ml White wine • 110g Mascarpone • 1 tsp Black pepper • 75g Unsalted butter, softened • 50g Parmesan, freshly grated

Bring the wine to the boil in a small, thick-bottomed pan. Reduce the heat and simmer until the wine is reduced by half. Add the gorgonzola bit by bit, stirring to melt the cheese into the wine. When the sauce is smooth, add the mascarpone, continue to simmer until you have a thick creamy sauce.

Cook the tagliatelle in boiling salted water until al dente. Drain, return to the saucepan, add the butter and toss to combine, then stir in the gorgonzola sauce and serve with the Parmesan.

22 Tagliatelle with asparagus

340g Dried egg tagliatelle • 1 kg Sprue asparagus, tough ends snapped off • 1 Garlic clove, peeled and crushed • 400ml Crème fraîche • 200g Parmesan, freshly grated, plus extra for serving • 2 Large egg yolks

Half fill a medium saucepan with water and place a metal bowl over it – the bowl should not touch the water. Bring to the boil.

Rub the garlic around the bowl. Add the crème fraîche, Parmesan and egg yolks and place over the saucepan. Heat, stirring all the time. Cook for 15 minutes until the sauce thickens. Season.

Slice the asparagus diagonally. Cook the tagliatelle in boiling salted water for 1 minute, then add the asparagus and cook until the pasta and asparagus are al dente. Drain, place in a warm bowl and pour over the sauce. Serve with extra Parmesan.

Tagliatelle with asparagus (Recipe 22)

CHAPTER THREE
VEGETARIAN SAUCES

23 Orecchiette with broccoli and olives • 24 Penne with asparagus carbonara • 25 Penne all'arrabbiata 26 Penne with aubergine, tomato and mozzarella 27 Penne with tomato and nutmeg • 28 Penne with zucchini and mint • 29 Conchiglie with tomato and dried porcini • 30 Penne with dried porcini, tomatoes and cream • 31 Penne with balsamic vinegar • 32 Taglierini with quick tomato sauce • 33 Taglierini with slow-cooked tomato sauce • 34 Spaghetti with ginger and tomato 35 Spaghetti with peppers, tomatoes and capers 36 Spaghetti with zucchini, capers and tomatoes 37 Spaghetti, boiled tomato sauce with celery and carrots • 38 Spaghetti with tomato purée 39 Tagliatelle with asparagus and spring herbs 40 Tagliatelle with fresh artichokes • 41 Linguine with broad beans • 42 Tagliatelle with dried porcini and sage • 43 Tagliatelle with girolle mushrooms 44 Pappardelle with leeks and porcini 45 Spaghetti with garlic, chilli, parsley and lemon 46 Tagliatelle with fresh figs and chilli • 47 Farfalle with grilled aubergine and zucchini • 48 Penne with deep-fried zucchini • 49 Farfalle with cavolo nero

23 Orecchiette with broccoli and olives

350g Orecchiette • 1kg Purple sprouting broccoli, flower heads and smaller leaves only • 100g Black olives, stoned • 2 Small red onions, peeled and finely sliced • 2 Garlic cloves, peeled and finely sliced • 2 Dried red chillies, crumbled • 1 tsp Fennel seeds, crushed • 3 tbs Roughly chopped flat-leaf parsley • 60g Pine nuts • 100g Pecorino, freshly grated • Extra virgin olive oil

Cut the larger broccoli heads into smaller pieces. Cook the broccoli in boiling salted water for 5 minutes. Drain, reserving 100ml of the water.

Heat 2 tbs of olive oil in a thick-bottomed pan and gently fry the onions until lightly golden. Add the garlic, chillies and fennel seeds, fry briefly, then add the parsley. Cook for 2 minutes, then add the broccoli and the reserved water. Continue to cook until the broccoli is broken up into a sauce. Add 3 tbs of olive oil, season and stir well.

Separately, fry the olives and pine nuts briefly in 1 tbs of olive oil.

Cook the orecchiette in boiling salted water until al dente. Drain, add to the broccoli sauce, then stir in the olives and pine nuts and half the pecorino. Serve with the remaining pecorino sprinkled over.

24 Penne with asparagus carbonara

350g Penne • 1kg Asparagus, tough ends snapped off • 150g Unsalted butter • 3 tbs Thyme leaves • 8 Egg yolks • 100g Parmesan, freshly grated

Cut off the tips of the asparagus and slice the remainder of the stalk at an angle, the same length as the penne.

Bring 2 saucepans of water to the boil and add salt. Cook the asparagus stalks in one of the pans, adding the tips after 2 minutes. Cook together for a further 3 minutes, then drain. »

« Melt the butter in a large frying pan. Add the thyme and as soon as it wilts, add the asparagus.

Cook the penne in the other pan until al dente, 9-12 minutes, according to size.

Beat the egg yolks with a fork and season lightly. Add half the Parmesan and mix.

Drain the penne and add to the warm asparagus. Add the egg mixture and toss to coat the penne evenly. Serve with the remaining Parmesan sprinkled over.

---

25   Penne all'arrabbiata

350g Penne • 4 Garlic cloves, peeled and cut in half • 4 Dried red chillies • 3 tbs Basil leaves • 750g Plum tomatoes, skinned and roughly chopped • Extra virgin olive oil

Heat 3 tbs of olive oil in a thick-bottomed pan. Add the garlic and fry gently. After 1 minute, add the whole chillies, then continue to fry until the garlic is lightly brown. Remove it with the chillies and save. Add the basil to the hot oil for a few moments to add flavour, then remove and save. Finally, add the tomatoes to the flavoured oil with 1 tsp of sea salt and cook gently for 10 minutes.

Cook the penne in boiling salted water until al dente. Drain, add to the tomato sauce, toss to coat and stir in the garlic, chillies and basil. Serve with olive oil drizzled over.

26 Penne with aubergine, tomato and mozzarella

350g Penne • 2 Aubergines, thinly sliced • 500g Plum tomatoes, skinned and roughly chopped • 250g Mozzarella, freshly grated • 2 Garlic cloves, peeled and thinly sliced • 3 tbs Finely chopped flat-leaf parsley • 2 Dried red chillies, crumbled • Extra virgin olive oil

Lay the sliced aubergines on kitchen paper and sprinkle with sea salt. Leave for 20 minutes to allow the bitter juices to drain. Rinse in cold water and pat dry.

Heat 3 tbs of olive oil in a thick-bottomed pan. Add the garlic and parsley and cook until soft. Add the tomatoes and their juices, the chillies and 2 tsp of sea salt, and cook over a medium heat for 20 minutes.

Heat 4 tbs of olive oil in a large, thick-bottomed frying pan. Fry the aubergines in batches until brown and crisp on both sides. Drain on kitchen paper.

Cook the penne in boiling salted water until al dente. Drain, return to the pan and add the tomato sauce. Stir to coat, then add the aubergine and finally the mozzarella. Serve immediately.

Penne with aubergine, tomato and mozzarella (Recipe 26)

27 Penne with tomato and nutmeg

350g Penne • 1kg Cherry tomatoes, halved and squeezed of their juice and seeds • ½ Nutmeg, freshly grated • 100g Unsalted butter • 4 Garlic cloves, peeled and finely sliced • 2 tbs Basil leaves • 100g Pecorino, freshly grated, plus extra for serving

Melt half the butter in a thick-bottomed pan. Add the garlic and cook until softened and lightly brown. Add the tomatoes and 1 tsp of sea salt and simmer gently for 15 minutes, stirring to break up the tomatoes. When it reduces to a sauce, add the nutmeg and cook for 3 or 4 minutes to combine the flavours. Check the seasoning. Add the basil and remove from the heat.

Cook the penne in boiling salted water until al dente. Drain, return to the pan and add the remaining butter and the pecorino. Stir to combine, then add the tomato sauce. Serve with the extra pecorino sprinkled over.

28 Penne with zucchini and mint

350g Penne • 1.5kg Zucchini, trimmed of stalks and tips • 4 tbs Mint leaves • 150g Unsalted butter • 2 Garlic cloves, peeled and finely chopped • 100g Parmesan, freshly grated

Cut the zucchini in half lengthways and then across in roughly 1cm pieces.

Melt half the butter in a thick-bottomed pan, add the zucchini and fry until soft and beginning to brown. Add the garlic, season generously and continue to cook, stirring to break up the zucchini. Add 2 tbs of hot water to lubricate the sauce. When the zucchini are soft, after about 20 minutes, mash half with a fork and add the remaining butter. Chop the mint and stir into the sauce.

Cook the penne in boiling salted water until al dente. Drain and add to the zucchini sauce. Toss together and serve with the Parmesan sprinkled over.

29 Conchiglie with tomato and dried porcini

350g Conchiglie • 2 x 400g Tins of peeled plum tomatoes, drained of their juices • 50g Dried porcini mushrooms, soaked in 200ml hot water for 15 minutes • 4 Garlic cloves, peeled and finely sliced • 100g Unsalted butter • 2 tbs Chopped flat-leaf parsley • 50g Parmesan, freshly grated • Extra virgin olive oil

Heat 1 tbs of oil in a thick-bottomed pan and fry half the garlic in it until soft. Add the tomatoes and season. Cook over a medium heat for 20 minutes, breaking up the tomatoes as they reduce to a sauce.

Drain the porcini, keeping back the water. Rinse the now-soft porcini in a sieve under a running tap to remove any grit. Strain the soaking liquid through a sieve lined with kitchen paper.

Melt the butter in a thick-bottomed saucepan, add the remaining garlic and fry until soft. Add the porcini and fry for 2 minutes. Add half of the strained porcini water and simmer for 15 minutes, stirring until it has been absorbed and the porcini are cooked. If the porcini are not soft add the remaining porcini water and continue to simmer for another 15 minutes. Stir in the parsley and add to the tomato sauce.

Cook the conchiglie in boiling salted water until al dente. Drain and stir the pasta into the sauce. Drizzle with olive oil and serve with the Parmesan.

30 Penne with dried porcini, tomatoes and cream

350g Penne • 50g Dried porcini mushrooms, soaked in 150ml hot water for 15 minutes • 400g Tin of peeled plum tomatoes, drained of their juices • 100ml Double cream • 80g Unsalted butter • 2 Garlic cloves, peeled and finely sliced • 1 Dried red chilli, crumbled • 2 tbs Finely chopped flat-leaf parsley • 50g Parmesan, freshly grated

Drain the porcini, keeping back the water. Rinse the now-soft porcini in a sieve under a running tap to remove any grit. Strain the soaking liquid through a sieve lined with kitchen paper. .

Melt the butter in a thick-bottomed pan and add the garlic, chilli and parsley. Fry gently until the garlic is soft, then add the porcini. Stir and cook for 2 minutes, then add the soaking liquid a little at a time – it will be absorbed very quickly. Continue cooking until all the liquid is absorbed and the porcini are soft and juicy. Add the tomatoes, chop them up into the porcini and cook over a medium heat for at least 30 minutes until the sauce thickens. Season. Stir in the cream, turn up the heat and boil for 2 minutes to combine the flavours.

Cook the penne in boiling salted water until al dente. Drain, add to the sauce and toss. Stir in half the Parmesan and serve with the remainder.

Penne with dried porcini, tomatoes and cream (Recipe 30)

31 Penne with balsamic vinegar

350g Penne • 4 tbs Traditional balsamic vinegar • 2 x 400g Tins of peeled plum tomatoes, drained of their juices • 2 Garlic cloves, peeled and sliced • 3 tbs Basil leaves • 180g Unsalted butter, cut into small pieces • 100g Parmesan, freshly grated • Extra virgin olive oil

Heat 2 tbs of olive oil in a thick-bottomed pan and fry the garlic in it until light brown. Add the tomatoes and season. Cook gently for 30 minutes, then stir in the basil.

Cook the penne in boiling salted water until al dente, then drain and return to the pan. Add the butter and heat gently. When the butter has melted, add the vinegar and toss for 1 minute to colour the penne. Add half the Parmesan and then stir in the tomato sauce. Serve with the remaining Parmesan.

32 Taglierini with quick tomato sauce

350g Dried egg taglierini • 2 x 400g Tins of plum tomatoes, drained of their juices • 3 Garlic cloves, peeled and finely sliced • Handful of basil leaves• Extra virgin olive oil

Heat 1-2 tbs of oil in a thick-bottomed pan, and fry the garlic until soft. Add the tomatoes and some sea salt, and cook fiercely, stirring constantly to prevent the tomatoes from sticking. As they cook, the tomatoes will release their juices. When this liquid has evaporated, add 1tbs olive oil, the basil and test for seasoning. Cook the taglierini in boiling salted water until al dente. Drain and add to the sauce, and toss to combine. Serve with olive oil drizzled over.

33 Taglierini with slow-cooked tomato sauce

350g Dried egg taglierini • 2 x 400g Tins of plum tomatoes, drained of their juices • 2 Medium red onions, peeled and sliced as thinly as possible • 2 Garlic cloves, peeled and finely sliced • Extra virgin olive oil

Heat 3tbs of olive oil in a thick-bottomed saucepan. Add the onions. Reduce the heat and cook until they are very soft. This will take at least 30 minutes. After 25 minutes add the garlic and allow to soften into the onions. Add the tomatoes and stir to break them up. Season with salt and continue to cook slowly, stirring occasionally, for at least 1 hour. The sauce will be dark red and extremely thick, with no juice at all. Cook the taglierini in boiling salted water until al dente. Drain and add to the sauce, and toss to combine.

34 Spaghetti with ginger and tomato

350g Spaghetti • 80g Fresh root ginger, peeled and finely sliced • 2 x 400g Tins of peeled plum tomatoes, drained of their juices • 4 Garlic cloves, peeled and finely sliced • 3 Dried red chillies, crumbled • Juice of 1 lemon • 150g Ricotta salata or aged pecorino, freshly grated • 3 tbs Chopped marjoram • Extra virgin olive oil

Heat 3 tbs of olive oil in a thick-bottomed pan and fry the garlic until soft. Add the ginger and chillies and cook until lightly brown. Add the tomatoes and season. Cook over a medium heat, stirring from time to time, breaking up the tomatoes to make a thick sauce. This will take 30 minutes. Pass the sauce through a mouli.

Cook the spaghetti in boiling salted water until al dente. Drain and return to the saucepan. Over a low heat, add 2 tbs of olive oil and the lemon juice and toss. Stir in half the ricotta or pecorino, the tomato and the marjoram. Serve with the remaining ricotta or pecorino sprinkled over.

35 Spaghetti with peppers, tomatoes and capers

350g Spaghetti • 2 Peppers, red and/or yellow, grilled and skinned (see note) • 500g Ripe plum tomatoes,

*skinned and roughly chopped • 50g Salted capers,
rinsed of all their salt • 5 Garlic cloves, 3 finely sliced, 2
peeled but left whole • 8 Anchovy fillets • 2 Dried red
chillies, crumbled • 2 tbs Red wine vinegar •
½ Ciabatta loaf, all crusts removed • 2 tbs Chopped
flat-leaf parsley • Extra virgin olive oil*

Roughly chop the peppers.

Heat 2 tbs of olive oil in a medium, thick-bottomed
pan. Add the sliced garlic and, when lightly coloured,
add the anchovies and chillies. Reduce the heat and
stir to break up the anchovies. Add the tomatoes and
some salt. Simmer gently for 30 minutes or until you
have a thick sauce. Add the peppers, capers and
vinegar, mix well and remove from the heat.

Pulse-chop the ciabatta in a food processor to make
coarse breadcrumbs.

Heat 100ml of olive oil in a small saucepan, add the 2
whole garlic cloves, and when golden brown, remove
with a slotted spoon. Add the breadcrumbs to the
hot, flavoured oil, stir and cook for 1-2 minutes, until
crisp and brown. Drain on kitchen paper.

Cook the spaghetti in boiling salted water until al
dente, drain and return to the saucepan. Add the
tomato sauce and heat briefly, tossing the pasta to
combine with the sauce. Stir in the parsley, test for
seasoning, and serve with the breadcrumbs on top.

*To skin peppers, grill them whole until black on all sides.
Place in a plastic bag, seal and leave to cool. When cool,
remove the blackened skin, then scrape out the seeds
and fibres.*

Spaghetti with peppers, tomatoes and capers (Recipe 35)

36 Spaghetti with zucchini, capers and tomatoes

350g Spaghetti • 400g Zucchini • 3 tbs Salted capers, rinsed of all their salt • 250g Cherry tomatoes, halved and squeezed, reserving the juice • 2 Dried red chillies, crumbled • 2 tsp Dried oregano • 2 Garlic cloves, peeled and finely chopped • 2 tbs White wine vinegar • 2 tbs Roughly chopped fresh oregano • Extra virgin olive oil

Combine the tomatoes with their juice and add the capers, chillies, dried oregano and garlic. Stir in 3 tbs of olive oil and the vinegar, then season.

Slice the zucchini into 5mm discs, then cut each disc into sticks 5mm wide. Heat 3 tbs of olive oil in a thick-bottomed pan, add the zucchini and fry until lightly browned.

Cook the spaghetti in boiling salted water until al dente, then drain. Add to the tomato mixture and stir in the zucchini. Scatter with the fresh oregano and drizzle with olive oil.

37 Spaghetti, boiled tomato sauce with celery and carrots

350g Spaghetti • 400g Tin of peeled plum tomatoes • 500g Ripe plum tomatoes, skinned and roughly chopped • 1 Celery heart, cut into quarters • 2 Carrots, cut in half lengthways • 2 Garlic cloves,

peeled • 1 Red onion, peeled and cut into quarters •
2 tbs Basil leaves • 1 Dried red chilli, crumbled •
Extra virgin olive oil

Put all the vegetables into a saucepan with the tinned
tomatoes and their juice, season and bring to the boil.
Turn the heat down and simmer gently for 45
minutes, until the vegetables are soft. Cool and passed
through a mouli. Heat the sauce and add the basil and
chilli. Stir in 2 tbs of olive oil.

Cook the spaghetti in boiling salted water until al
dente, then drain and add the sauce. Serve with olive
oil drizzled over.

38 Spaghetti with tomato purée

350g Spaghetti • 2kg Ripe plum tomatoes • 1 Red or
white onion, peeled and grated on the coarse side of a
cheese grater • 3 tbs Basil leaves • Extra virgin olive oil

Slit the skin of each tomato down one side, then
cook in boiling salted water for half a minute. Remove
with a slotted spoon and put into a bowl of cold
water. When cool enough to handle, remove the
skins. Make a cut lengthways down the side of each
tomato and put in a colander over a bowl to drain off
the juice.

Push the tomato flesh through a mouli and, if the
purée seems too thick, stir in a little of the juice
collected. Test for seasoning, adding salt if necessary.
This purée is suitable to store for the winter: place in »

« sterilised jam jars, pour over 1 tbs of olive oil and cover loosely with lids. Place the jam jars in a saucepan and boil for 5 minutes. Allow to cool, then hermetically seal.

To make the sauce, put the onion into a small saucepan and cover with 2cm water. Heat gently and simmer until the water has evaporated. Add 6 tbs of tomato purée and continue to simmer until the sauce is thick and sweet, about 25 minutes. Season.

Cook the spaghetti in boiling salted water until al dente. Drain, stir into the sauce, then add the basil and a drizzle of olive oil.

39 Tagliatelle with asparagus and spring herbs

350g Tagliatelle • 500g Sprue asparagus, tough ends trimmed • 4 tbs Roughly chopped herbs: basil, mint, marjoram, parsley • 200ml Double cream • 3 Garlic cloves, 1 finely sliced, 2 peeled but left whole • 50g Unsalted butter • 75g Parmesan, freshly grated • Extra virgin olive oil

Cut the asparagus stalks into 2cm slices at an angle, cutting off the tips. Blanch the stalks for 2 minutes in boiling salted water. Remove with a slotted spoon. Place on a board and chop roughly. Scatter with sea salt. Add the tips to the pan and blanch for 1 minute. Drain.

Bring the cream to the boil with the whole garlic cloves and simmer until the garlic is soft, about 10 minutes. Mash the garlic into the cream and season.

Heat 2 tbs of olive oil with the butter and fry the sliced garlic until lightly browned. Add the chopped herbs, then the chopped asparagus stalks, and stir to combine. Add the cream and bring to the boil, then remove from the heat.

Cook the pasta in boiling salted water until al dente. Drain and return to the pan. Add the asparagus sauce, the tips and half the Parmesan. Toss to combine. Serve with the remaining Parmesan.

40 Tagliatelle with fresh artichokes

*350g Tagliatelle • 6 Globe artichokes • ½ Lemon •
3 Garlic cloves, peeled • 3 tbs Flat-leaf parsley •
50g Unsalted butter • 200ml Double cream •
50g Parmesan, freshly grated • Extra virgin olive oil*

To prepare the artichokes, break off the outside leaves until you get to the tender pale leaves. Cut off the tips of the remaining leaves and peel the fibres from the stalks. Cut off the stalks 3cm from the base of the artichokes and reserve. Halve the artichokes lengthways through the stalk and remove the choke. This is easily done with a teaspoon.

Very finely slice the artichoke hearts and put in a bowl of water with the lemon half. Finely chop the garlic together with the peeled artichoke stalks and the parsley.

Melt the butter with 2 tbs of olive oil in a thick-bottomed frying pan. Add the chopped stalk mixture and fry gently until soft, 2-3 minutes. Add 100ml boiling water and season. Drain and pat dry the sliced hearts, then add to the pan. Stir together and cook for 10 minutes or until the artichokes are soft, adding a tablespoon of hot water if too dry. Stir in the cream, bring to the boil, then remove from the heat.

Cook the tagliatelle in boiling salted water until al dente, then drain, keeping back a little of the pasta water. Add the pasta to the sauce and toss to combine. Add a little of the retained water if the sauce is too thick. Serve with the Parmesan.

41   Linguine with broad beans

*350g Linguine • 2kg Broad beans in their pods
(podded weight, 800g – choose young pods with
smallish beans inside) • 1 Red onion, peeled and finely
chopped • 2 Garlic cloves, peeled and finely chopped •
3 tbs Chopped flat-leaf parsley • 60g Aged pecorino,
freshly grated • Extra virgin olive oil*

Heat 3 tbs of olive oil in a thick-bottomed pan, add
the onion and cook gently until soft. Add the garlic
and half the parsley and cook until the onion and
garlic have changed colour. Season. Add the podded
broad beans and 100ml hot water, then cover and
simmer for 8 minutes, until the beans are tender.

Pulse-chop half the beans to a coarse purée and mix
with the whole beans. Stir in the remaining parsley.

Cook the linguine in boiling salted water until al
dente. Drain, add to the sauce and toss to coat the
pasta. Stir in half the pecorino and drizzle with a little
olive oil. Serve with the remaining pecorino.

Linguine with broad beans (Recipe 41)

42 Tagliatelle with dried porcini and sage

350g Dried egg tagliatelle • 35g Dried porcini mushrooms, soaked in 200ml hot water for 20 minutes • 8 Sage leaves, finely sliced • 100g Unsalted butter • 2 Garlic cloves, peeled and finely sliced • 1 Dried red chilli, crumbled • 4 tbs Double cream • Zest and juice of 1 lemon • 50g Parmesan, freshly grated

Drain the porcini, keeping back the water. Rinse the now-soft porcini in a sieve under a running tap to remove any grit. Roughly chop. Strain the soaking liquid through a sieve lined with kitchen paper.

Melt the butter in a thick-bottomed pan, add the garlic, sage and chilli and fry gently until the garlic is lightly coloured. Add the porcini and stir to combine. Cook for 15 minutes, adding a few tablespoons of the soaking liquid to keep the porcini moist if necessary. When the porcini are soft, stir in the cream, lemon zest and juice, then season.

Cook the tagliatelle in boiling salted water until al dente, then drain. Add to the sauce and toss. Stir in the Parmesan.

43 Tagliatelle with girolle mushrooms

*350g Dried egg tagliatelle • 500g Fresh girolles •
3 Garlic cloves, peeled and finely sliced • 2 tbs Finely
chopped flat-leaf parsley • 100g Unsalted butter,
softened • 1 tbs Lemon juice • 100g Parmesan, freshly
grated • Extra virgin olive oil*

Carefully clean the girolles, brushing off moss and
earth. Trim off the ends of the stems. Tear them in half
and then in half again, keeping the stalks attached.

Heat 2 tbs of olive oil in a thick-bottomed frying pan
until smoking. Add the girolles and toss as you cook
them, for 5 minutes. Add the garlic and continue to
cook until the garlic is soft, stirring all the time to
prevent the garlic from burning, and until the girolles
are tender and the juices absorbed. Stir in the parsley
and season.

Cook the tagliatelle in boiling salted water until al
dente. Drain, return to the pan and add the butter
and the girolles. Toss with the lemon juice and half the
Parmesan. Serve with the remaining Parmesan.

*The girolles season begins at the end of July and
continues through August. The best girolles come from
Scotland. If picking your own, check for authenticity using
a good illustrated reference book, such as Roger Philips'
Mushrooms and Other Funghi of Great Britain
and Europe.*

44 Pappardelle with leeks and porcini

350g Dried egg pappardelle • 500g Leeks, peeled of their outer layers and cut on the diagonal into slices 3cm thick • 50g Dried porcini mushrooms, soaked in 150ml hot water for 20 minutes • 100g Unsalted butter • 2 Garlic cloves, peeled and finely sliced • 2 tbs Thyme leaves • 50g Parmesan, freshly grated • Extra virgin olive oil

Drain the porcini, keeping back the water. Rinse the now-soft porcini in a sieve under a running tap to remove any grit then roughly chop. Strain the soaking liquid through a sieve lined with kitchen paper.

Heat 2 tbs of olive oil with half the butter in a thick-bottomed frying pan. Add the garlic and cook until soft. Add the porcini and stir and fry for 1 minute, then add a little of the porcini liquid to keep them moist, adding more as the liquid is absorbed. Cook in this way for 20 minutes. Season.

In a separate frying pan, heat 2 tbs of oil with half the remaining butter. When hot, add the leeks and the thyme. Season and stir-fry briefly. Add 3 tbs of boiling water, then cook over a high heat until the liquid is reduced, about 5 minutes. Add the porcini to the leeks and toss together.

Cook the pappardelle in boiling salted water until al dente, then drain and add to the sauce. Stir in the remaining butter and the Parmesan.

45 Spaghetti with garlic, chilli, parsley and lemon

350g Spaghetti • 6 Garlic cloves, peeled and finely sliced • 3 Dried red chillies, crumbled • 4 tbs Chopped flat-leaf parsley • Juice of ½ lemon • Extra virgin olive oil

Heat 100ml olive oil gently in a thick-bottomed pan. Add the garlic and fry until soft and golden, then add the parsley and chillies and season. Stir in the lemon juice.

Cook the spaghetti in boiling salted water until al dente. Drain and add to the garlic sauce. Toss to combine.

46 Tagliatelle with fresh figs and chilli

350g Dried egg tagliatelle • 8 Black figs, stalks removed, cut into quarters • 2 Dried red chillies, crumbled • Zest of 2 lemons • Juice of 1 lemon • 100ml Double cream • 50g Parmesan, freshly grated • Extra virgin olive oil

Mix the lemon zest and juice into the cream and season. Cook the tagliatelle in boiling salted water until al dente.

While the pasta is cooking, heat a frying pan large enough to hold the figs in one layer. Add 2 tbs of olive oil and, when smoking, place the figs in the pan, turning them immediately to caramelise on each side. Remove from the heat, sprinkle with the chillies and season.

Drain the pasta, return to the pan, then stir in the cream mixture and toss together. Add the figs and serve with the Parmesan sprinkled over.

47 Farfalle with grilled aubergine and zucchini

350g Farfalle • *1 Large pale aubergine, cut into 1cm slices* • *500g Zucchini, cut into 1cm slices lengthways* • *2 tbs Chopped flat-leaf parsley* • *1 tbs Chopped mint leaves* • *Juice of 1 lemon* • *Extra virgin olive oil*

Pangrattato
½ Ciabatta loaf, crust removed, made into crumbs • *2 Garlic cloves, peeled*

Place the aubergine slices in a colander and sprinkle with sea salt. Leave for 30 minutes then rinse in cold water and pat dry.

Preheat a griddle pan to very hot. Grill the aubergines on both sides until brown and soft in the centre, then cut each slice into 1cm ribbons. Grill the zucchini on both sides and cut into pieces the same size as the aubergine.

Put the herbs into a bowl. Add the aubergines and zucchini, and season. Mix the lemon juice with three times its volume of olive oil, pour over the vegetables and toss.

Make the pangrattato (see Recipe 55).

Cook the farfalle in boiling salted water until al dente. Drain, keeping back 2-3 tbs of the water. Return the pasta to the saucepan, add the vegetable mixture and stir over a low heat for 2-3 minutes. Serve covered with the pangrattato.

Farfalle with grilled aubergine and zucchini (Recipe 47)

48   Penne with deep-fried zucchini

350g Penne • 750g Small zucchini, cut into fine dice • 5 Egg yolks • 1 Egg white • 100g Aged pecorino, freshly grated • 2 Dried red chillies, crumbled • 3 tbs Roughly torn basil leaves • Extra virgin olive oil

Mix the egg yolks and egg white together. Season and stir in half the pecorino.

Heat 250ml olive oil in a thick-bottomed pan and fry the zucchini in batches, one layer at a time, until brown and crisp. Drain on kitchen paper.

Cook the penne in boiling salted water until al dente. Drain, return to the pan and add the egg mixture. Toss to coat, then add the zucchini, chillies, basil and pecorino.

49   Farfalle with cavolo nero

350g Farfalle • 1kg Cavolo nero leaves, stripped from their stalks • 200ml Extra virgin olive oil • 4 Garlic cloves, peeled • 50g Parmesan, freshly grated

Cook the cavolo nero in boiling salted water with the garlic until tender, about 15 minutes. Drain, keeping the garlic and 3 tbs of the water. Cool for 10 minutes. Put in a food processor and pulse-chop to a rough purée, then start adding the olive oil, keeping back 2 tbs. The consistency should be creamy. Season.

Cook the farfalle in boiling salted water. Drain and return to the saucepan. Stir in the purée and the retained pasta water; each piece of farfalle should be thickly coated. Then add the remaining oil to loosen the sauce. Serve with the Parmesan.

Buy extra virgin olive oil that comes from a named estate and displays the year it was pressed on the label. In Europe the olives are pressed from the end of October through to January. Olive oil changes in the bottle throughout the year, becoming less spicy in taste as it ages.

The first pressed oil from the Tuscan region of Italy where they choose to pick the olives green has a strong, peppery taste and is a bright green colour. Ligurian oil is picked when the olives are riper, and has a softer, fruitier flavour and a golden colour. Puglian and Sicilian oils have a pronounced spiciness and are rich and nutty in flavour. Choose a Tuscan oil for this recipe and make it in November when the cavolo nero has had its first frost and the flavour is superb.

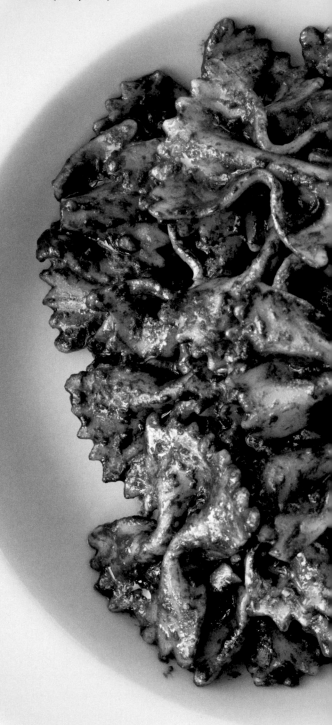

Farfalle with cavolo nero (Recipe 49)

CHAPTER FOUR
FISH SAUCES

50 Orecchiette with clams and broccoli • 51 Penne with mussels and zucchini • 52 Ditaloni, mussels and cream • 53 Spirali with clams and prawns 54 Linguine with sardines • 55 Bucatini with anchovies and pangrattato • 56 Linguine with crab, red chilli and extra virgin olive oil • 57 Orecchiette with scallops and rocket • 58 Tagliatelle with brown shrimps and peas • 59 Linguine with clams, white asparagus and cinnamon • 60 Linguine with crab and fresh fennel • 61 Linguine with sardines and saffron • 62 Spaghetti from le Marche 63 Spaghetti with marinated lobster • 64 Spaghetti with clams and Prosecco • 65 Spaghetti in the bag 66 Spaghetti with roasted red mullet and olives 67 Spaghetti with squid and zucchini • 68 Taglierini with red mullet and bay • 69 Tagliatelle with langoustines and ricotta • 70 Taglierini with clams and fried zucchini • 71 Spaghetti with bottarga

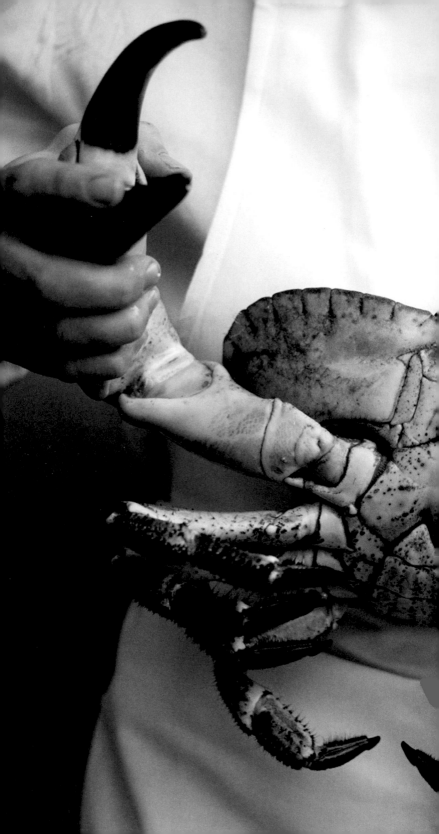

50 Orecchiette with clams and broccoli

350g Orecchiette • 1kg Clams, scrubbed • 500g Purple sprouting broccoli, divided into spears, tough stalks and leaves discarded • 3 Garlic cloves, peeled and finely sliced • 4 Anchovy fillets • 1 Dried red chilli, crumbled • 1 tsp Fennel seeds, roughly ground • 1 Fresh red chilli, cut in half lengthways, de-seeded and chopped • 2 tbs Chopped flat-leaf parsley • 150ml White wine • Extra virgin olive oil

Discard any open clams that do not close when tapped on the side of the sink.

Cook the broccoli in boiling salted water until very tender, keeping the broccoli wet when draining.

Heat 2 tbs of olive oil in a thick-bottomed pan. Add half the garlic and fry until soft. Over a low heat, add the anchovies, breaking them up into the oil, then season, adding the dried chilli and the fennel seeds. Add the broccoli and any residual liquid and cook, blending together to make the sauce.

Heat 2 tbs of olive oil in a large pan. Add the fresh chilli, the remaining garlic and the parsley and fry until brown. Add the clams and wine, then cover and cook over a high heat, shaking the pan, for 3 minutes or until all the clams are open. Drain, reserving the liquid.

Remove the clams from their shells. Add to the broccoli with enough of the cooking liquid to thin the sauce.

Cook the orecchiette in boiling salted water until al dente. Drain and add to the sauce. Toss together, adding more clam juice if necessary. Serve with olive oil.

---

51 Penne with mussels and zucchini

350g Penne • 1kg Mussels, scrubbed (small ones are best for this recipe) • 500g Zucchini, cut into 5mm discs at an angle • 2 Garlic cloves, peeled and sliced • 2 Dried red chillies, crumbled • 3 tbs Basil leaves • 50g Parmesan, freshly grated • Extra virgin olive oil

Discard any open mussels that do not close when tapped on the side of the sink.

Cut each zucchini disc into 3 sticks. Scatter with salt and leave to drain for 15 minutes. Pat dry.

Heat 3 tbs of olive oil in a thick-bottomed pan, add the zucchini and fry until lightly browned. Add the garlic, mussels and chillies and season. Stir and cover the pan. Cook over a high heat for 4 minutes, shaking the pan, until all the mussels have opened. Remove half of the mussels from their shells and return to the pan. Stir in the basil.

Cook the penne in boiling salted water until al dente. Drain and stir into the mussels. Serve with the Parmesan.

Penne with mussels and zucchini (Recipe 51)

52   Ditaloni, mussels and cream

*350g Ditaloni • 1.5kg Small mussels, scrubbed •
150ml Double cream • 120ml White wine • 150g
Unsalted butter • 2 Garlic cloves, peeled and finely
chopped • 4 tbs Flat-leaf parsley, finely chopped •
1 tbs Extra virgin olive oil*

Heat half the butter with the olive oil in a large, thick-
bottomed saucepan. Add the garlic. When lightly
coloured add the mussels and wine and season.
Cover and cook over a high heat until all the mussels
are open. Drain the mussels, keeping the liquid. When
cool, remove the mussels from their shells, discarding
the shells and any that haven't opened.

Heat the remaining butter in a small pan, add the
mussel juice and the cream. Cook gently to reduce to
a thick creamy sauce. Add the mussels and stir in the
parsley, test for seasoning.

Cook the ditaloni in boiling salted water until al
dente, drain and add to the sauce. Toss together
briefly over a low heat and serve in bowls.

*Ditaloni is a small tubular pasta. Short penne can be
used as an alternative. Buy small mussels so that they
are the same size as the pasta.*

53   Spirali with clams and prawns

350g Spirali • 1kg Clams, scrubbed • 250g Cooked peeled prawns • 3 Garlic cloves, peeled and finely chopped • 150ml White wine • 100g Rocket, roughly chopped • 1 Fresh red chilli, cut in half lengthways, de-seeded and chopped • 2 Lemons, cut in half • Extra virgin olive oil

Discard any open clams that do not close when tapped on the side of the sink.

Heat 3 tbs of olive oil in a large, thick-bottomed pan and add the garlic. When lightly coloured, add the clams and wine, season and cover. Cook over a high heat until the clams open. Add the prawns, rocket and chilli and cover again to wilt the rocket. Keep warm.

Cook the spirali in boiling salted water until al dente. Drain and add to the clams. Toss together and serve with a drizzle of olive oil and the lemon halves.

Greenland frozen prawns are the best: cooked and frozen aboard the boats. The season is June, August, September and October. Not July, as then they are too soft. Prawns preserved in brine come from Norway and are good. The little brown shrimps (which you can substitute) mostly come from France and are sold whole, sometimes live, or cooked and peeled. They always have a good flavour.

54 Linguine with sardines

350g Linguine • 1kg Fresh sardines, scaled and filleted
• 2 Red onions, peeled and finely sliced • 3 Garlic
cloves, peeled and finely sliced • 1 tbs Fennel seeds,
ground • 2 Dried red chillies, crumbled • 2 tbs Roughly
chopped flat-leaf parsley • 150ml White wine •
2 Fennel bulbs, thinly sliced, green tops finely chopped
• 50g Pine nuts, salted and roasted until lightly
browned • 2 Lemons, cut in half • Extra virgin olive oil

Heat 4 tbs of olive oil in a large, thick-bottomed frying
pan, add the onions and cook gently until soft and
beginning to colour. Add the garlic and continue to
cook for a few minutes, then add the ground fennel
seed, chillies and parsley. Carefully place the sardine
fillets in one layer over the onion mixture. Add the
wine, season and cover. Heat briefly until the sardines
are cooked through – about 1½ minutes. Drizzle
with olive oil and scatter over the fennel tops.
Remove from the heat and keep warm.

Cook the linguine with the sliced fennel in boiling
salted water until al dente. Drain and add to the
sardines. Toss gently to mix together, trying not to
break up the sardines. Serve with the pine nuts on
top of each portion, with a drizzle of olive oil and a
lemon half.

55   Bucatini with anchovies and pangrattato

350g Bucatini • 14 Anchovy fillets • ½ Ciabatta loaf, all crust removed • 5 Garlic cloves, 3 finely sliced, 2 peeled but left whole • 2 Dried red chillies, crumbled • Zest and juice of 1 lemon • 2 tbs finely chopped flat-leaf parsley • Extra virgin olive oil

Make the pangrattato. Pulse-chop the ciabatta to coarse breadcrumbs. Heat 100ml olive oil and add the 2 whole garlic cloves. When they are golden brown, remove with a slotted spoon. Add the breadcrumbs to the hot, flavoured oil, stir and cook for 1-2 minutes, until crisp and brown. Drain on kitchen paper.

Gently heat 3 tbs of olive oil in a medium, thick-bottomed saucepan. Add the sliced garlic and, when soft and beginning to colour, stir in the anchovies, breaking them up to become liquid. Remove from the heat and season with the chillies and some black pepper. Add the lemon juice and stir to combine.

Cook the bucatini in boiling salted water until al dente, then drain and add to the anchovy sauce. Toss to coat evenly. Stir in the lemon zest and parsley. Serve with 2 tbs of pangrattato sprinkled over each plate.

Bucatini with anchovies and pangrattato (Recipe 55)

56 Linguine with crab, red chilli and extra virgin olive oil

350g Linguine • 800g Crab meat, white and brown • 3 Fresh red chillies, cut in half lengthways, de-seeded and finely chopped • 1 Garlic clove, peeled and ground to a paste with 1 tsp sea salt • Juice of 1 lemon, plus 1 lemon cut into quarters • 3 tbs Finely chopped flat-leaf parsley • Extra virgin olive oil

Stir the chillies, garlic, lemon juice and some black pepper into the crab meat, then loosen with olive oil.

Cook the linguine in boiling salted water until al dente. Drain, keeping back 3 tbs of the pasta water. Return to the pan, stir in the crab and toss to combine over a low heat. Add more lemon juice and olive oil if the sauce is too thick. When hot, add the parsley and serve with the lemon quarters.

57 Orecchiette with scallops and rocket

350g Orecchiette • 8 Large scallops, cut into quarters • 100g Rocket, roughly chopped • 500g Cherry tomatoes, halved and squeezed to remove juice and seeds • 2 Fresh red chillies, cut in half lengthways, de-seeded and finely sliced • 2 Garlic cloves, peeled and finely chopped • 1 Lemon, cut into quarters • Extra virgin olive oil

Put the tomatoes in a bowl, add the chillies, garlic and 2 tbs of olive oil and season generously.

Heat 1 tbs of olive oil in a small, thick-bottomed frying pan and add the scallops. Season and fry, turning the pieces over, until brown. Add the marinated tomatoes and stir over the heat briefly to combine.

Cook the orecchiette in boiling salted water until al dente. Drain and add to the scallops. Stir in the rocket and test for seasoning. Serve with a drizzled of olive oil and the lemon quarters.

58 Tagliatelle with brown shrimps and peas

350g Tagliatelle • 500g Brown shrimps, peeled • 500g Frozen peas • 150g Unsalted butter • 2 Garlic cloves, peeled and finely chopped • Juice of 2 lemons, plus 1 lemon cut into quarters • 2 tbs Chopped mint

Melt half the butter in a thick-bottomed saucepan and add the garlic. Fry until soft, then add the shrimps. Cook just to heat up the shrimps, season and stir in half the lemon juice. Remove from the heat.

Cook the peas in boiling salted water until al dente. Drain and add to the shrimps.

Cook the tagliatelle in boiling salted water until al dente. Drain and add to the shrimps. Stir in the remaining butter and lemon juice, and the mint. Toss to combine and melt the butter. Check the seasoning and serve with the lemon quarters.

Peeled brown shrimps come from Holland and are only fished in the North Sea. They are cooked in sea water the moment they are caught, then peeled and salted. After they are packed they must be consumed within 21 days.

59 Linguine with clams, white asparagus and cinnamon

350g Linguine • 1.5kg Clams, scrubbed • 500g White asparagus • 1.5cm Cinnamon stick, roughly broken • 200g Unsalted butter • 120ml White wine • 1 Lemon, cut into quarters

Discard any open clams that do not close when tapped on the side of the sink.

Snap the tough ends off the asparagus, peel the stems and then cut them into thin ribbons, using a vegetable peeler or a mandoline.

Slowly heat half the butter in a medium, thick-bottomed pan. Add the clams, cinnamon and wine, season and cover. Cook over a high heat until all the clams are open, about 3 minutes. Drain, reserving the liquid. Cool and remove half the clams from their shells. Return all the clams to the liquid.

Cook the linguine in boiling salted water for 6 minutes, then add the asparagus and cook for a further 6 minutes; the linguine will be al dente and the asparagus tender. Drain and add to the clams with the remaining butter. Toss together over a low heat. Serve with the lemon quarters.

60 Linguine with crab and fresh fennel

350g Linguine • 500g Crab meat, white and brown • 2 Fennel bulbs, finely sliced, green tops kept • 2 Garlic cloves, peeled and finely chopped • 1 tbs Fennel seeds, crushed • 2 Dried red chillies, crushed • Zest and juice of 1 lemon • Extra virgin olive oil

Heat 2 tbs of olive oil in a medium, thick-bottomed pan and add the garlic. When soft and beginning to colour, add the fennel seeds and chillies and season. Add the crab and stir to mix in the flavours, just to heat through. When warm, add the lemon zest and juice.

Cook the linguine in boiling salted water for 6 minutes, then add the sliced fennel and continue cooking until the pasta is al dente and the fennel tender. Drain, keeping a little of the pasta water. Add the linguine to the crab mixture and stir to coat each strand, adding a little of the pasta water to loosen the sauce. Season. Scatter over the fennel green tops and serve drizzled with olive oil.

61 Linguine with sardines and saffron

350g Linguine • 12 Fresh sardines, scaled and filleted • 1 tsp Saffron threads, soaked in 6 tbs boiling water • 2 Garlic cloves, peeled and finely sliced • 3 tbs Chopped flat-leaf parsley • 2 Dried red chillies, crumbled • 120ml White wine • 50g Pine nuts • 50g Raisins, soaked in 100ml hot water for 20 minutes • 1 Lemon, cut into quarters • Extra virgin olive oil

Heat 3 tbs of olive oil in a large, thick-bottomed frying pan. Add the garlic and parsley and cook until the garlic has softened. Add the sardine fillets in one layer, season with the chillies, salt and pepper, then add the wine and cover. Cook over a low heat for 2 minutes or until the sardines are just done.

In a small pan, lightly brown the pine nuts. Cook the linguine in boiling salted water until al dente, then drain and return to the saucepan. Add the saffron and its liquid, then stir in to colour the pasta. Drain the raisins and add to the pasta. Finally, gently fold in the sardines with the juices from the pan. Check for seasoning. Serve with the pine nuts scattered over and the lemon quarters.

62 Spaghetti from le Marche

350g Spaghetti • 2kg Mussels, scrubbed • 3 Garlic cloves, peeled and chopped • 150ml White wine • 1 Dried red chilli, crumbled • 1 tbs Dried oregano, flowers and leaves, stalks picked out • 1kg Ripe plum tomatoes, skinned and roughly chopped • 2 tbs Chopped fresh oregano • Juice of 1 lemon, plus 1 lemon cut into quarters • Extra virgin olive oil

Discard any open mussels that do not close when tapped on the side of the sink.

Heat 3 tbs of olive oil in a large, thick-bottomed pan. Add half the garlic, the mussels and the wine. Cover the pan and cook over a high heat for 2 minutes or until all the mussels have opened. Allow to cool, then drain, keeping the liquid. Remove the mussels from their shells and finely chop. Return the pulp to the liquid the mussels were cooked in.

In a separate pan heat 2 tbs of olive oil, then add the remaining garlic, the chilli and the dried oregano. When the garlic begins to colour, add the tomatoes and season. Simmer for 20 minutes. Stir to break up the tomatoes and reduce to a thick sauce. Add the mussels and their juice and the fresh oregano, then add the lemon juice and stir to combine.

Cook the spaghetti in boiling salted water until al dente. Drain, stir in the sauce and toss. Serve with a drizzle of olive oil and the lemon quarters.

63 Spaghetti with marinated lobster

350g Spaghetti • 2 x 750g Lobsters, cooked, all meat removed from the shells and claws • 2 Garlic cloves, peeled and crushed in 1 tbs sea salt • Juice of 3 lemons, plus 1 lemon cut into quarters • 2 Dried red chillies, crumbled • 3 tbs Finely chopped flat-leaf parsley • Extra virgin olive oil

Roughly chop the lobster meat, leaving some of the claw meat whole.

Mix the garlic with the lemon juice and stir in 120ml olive oil. Pour this mixture over the lobster meat, scatter over the chillies, then cover and leave to marinate for a minimum of 30 minutes.

Cook the spaghetti in boiling salted water until al dente. Drain, keeping back 2-3 tbs of the cooking water, and return to the pan. Add the lobster and the marinade. Heat through, stir in the parsley and check for seasoning. Serve with a drizzle of olive oil and the lemon quarters.

Spaghetti with marinated lobster (Recipe 63)

64 Spaghetti with clams and Prosecco

350g Spaghetti • 3kg Small clams, scrubbed • 350ml Prosecco • 3 Garlic cloves, peeled and finely sliced • 2 Dried red chillies, crumbled • I tsp Fennel seeds, crushed • 3 tbs Chopped flat-leaf parsley • I Lemon, cut into quarters • Extra virgin olive oil

Discard any open clams that do not close when tapped on the side of the sink.

Heat 2 tbs of olive oil in a large, thick-bottomed pan. Add the garlic and cook until light brown. Add the chillies and fennel seeds, stir to combine, then add the clams. Stir over a high heat for half a minute, add the Prosecco, season and cover. Cook until the clams open, about 3 minutes.

Cook the spaghetti in boiling salted water until al dente, then drain and add to the clam sauce. Stir together briefly over the heat. Remove any empty shells. Stir in the parsley and drizzle with I tbs of olive oil. Serve with the lemon quarters.

65 Spaghetti in the bag

350g Spaghetti • 4 Garlic cloves, peeled and finely chopped • 2 x 400g Tins of peeled plum tomatoes, drained of their juices • I Fresh red chilli, cut in half lenthways, de-seeded and finely sliced • 500g Cooked peeled prawns • Juice of I lemon, plus I lemon cut into

*quarters • 3 tbs Basil leaves • 120ml White wine •
Extra virgin olive oil*

Heat 2 tbs of olive oil in a thick-bottomed pan, add
half the garlic and cook until light brown. Add the
tomatoes and some sea salt. Simmer gently, stirring to
break up the tomatoes, for 20 minutes or until you
have a thick sauce.

Heat 3 tbs of olive oil in a separate thick-bottomed
frying pan and add the remaining garlic. When
coloured, add the chilli and prawns and toss together,
just long enough to heat the prawns. Add the lemon
juice and remove from the heat.

Preheat the oven to 200°C/Gas Mark 6.

Cook the spaghetti in boiling salted water for only 7
minutes, then drain. Put in a bowl and season. Add
3 tbs of olive oil and toss.

To make the bags, cut foil into four 50cm lengths.
Drizzle with olive oil. Divide the spaghetti into 4 and
place in the centre of each piece of foil. Spoon one
quarter of the tomato sauce, some prawns and a
quarter of the basil leaves over each. Scatter with sea
salt and black pepper. Bring the edges of the foil
together and fold to seal, leaving one side open. Pour
2 tbs of wine into each and seal.

Place the sealed bags on a tray in the oven and bake
for 6-8 minutes, until they inflate. Open each bag on a
plate and serve with a lemon quarter.

Spaghetti in the bag (Recipe 65)

66 Spaghetti with roasted red mullet and olives

350g Spaghetti • 2 x 500g Red mullet, scaled and filleted • 100g Small black olives, stoned • 500g Cherry tomatoes • 2 tbs Thyme leaves • 2 Dried red chillies, crumbled • 1 Lemon, cut into quarters • Extra virgin olive oil

Preheat the oven to 200°C/Gas Mark 6.

Prick each tomato with a small knife and place in a small baking dish in one layer. Season and drizzle with olive oil. Roast for 20 minutes, then add the olives and roast for a further 5 minutes.

Place the mullet in one layer in a separate shallow baking dish, sprinkle with the thyme and chillies and season. Drizzle with olive oil and roast in the oven for 5 minutes.

Cook the spaghetti in boiling salted water until al dente. Drain and return to the pan. Add the olives and tomatoes and their juices, then add the mullet and their juices and toss together. Serve with a drizzle of olive oil and the lemon quarters.

67 Spaghetti with squid and zucchini

*350g Spaghetti • 500g Squid • 500g Zucchini •
2 Dried red chillies, crumbled • I tbs Fennel seeds,
crushed • 3 Garlic cloves, peeled and very finely sliced
• 4 tbs Chopped marjoram • Zest and juice of
I lemon, plus I lemon cut into quarters • Extra virgin
olive oil*

Prepare the squid by pulling away the head and
tentacles from the body. Cut the tentacles off the
head and squeeze out the hard beak. Slit the body sac
down one side to open it out into a flat piece and
scrape away the soft interior pulp. Discard the quill.
Cut the body into fine 2cm strips. Separate the
tentacles. Wash and dry on kitchen paper.

Grate the zucchini at an angle on the large side of a
cheese grater. Sprinkle with salt and put in a colander
to drain for 15 minutes. Wash off the salt and pat dry.

Heat 3 tbs of olive oil in a large, thick-bottomed frying
pan. When smoking hot, add the squid. Stir briefly,
season, add the chillies and fennel seeds, then
immediately add the zucchini and garlic. Stir-fry for 5
minutes, just to brown the squid and soften the
zucchini. Add the marjoram and the lemon zest and
juice, then remove from the heat.

Cook the spaghetti in boiling salted water until al
dente, then drain and add to the squid. Toss to
combine. Serve with a drizzle of olive oil and the
lemon quarters.

68 Taglierini with red mullet and bay

350g Dried egg taglierini • 2 x 500g Red mullet, scaled and filleted • 6 Fresh bay leaves, pounded in a pestle and mortar, stems discarded • 100g Unsalted butter • 2 Garlic cloves, peeled and finely chopped • 2 x 400g Tins of peeled plum tomatoes, put through a mouli with their juices • 3 tbs Red wine vinegar • Zest and juice of 1 large lemon • 3 tbs Finely chopped flat-leaf parsley • Extra virgin olive oil

Finely slice across each red mullet fillet into 3mm strips.

Melt the butter in a thick-bottomed saucepan, add the garlic and bay and cook gently until the garlic is coloured. Add the tomato pulp and season. Add the vinegar and simmer gently for 30 minutes, stirring from time to time. Add the mullet and the lemon juice, stir gently and cook for 1 minute to melt the mullet into the sauce. Stir in the lemon zest and parsley.

Cook the taglierini in boiling salted water until al dente. Drain, add to the sauce and toss to combine. Serve drizzled with olive oil.

69 Tagliatelle with langoustines and ricotta

350g Tagliatelle • 2kg Langoustines • 300g Ricotta • Zest and juice of 1 lemon, plus 1 lemon cut into quarters • 2 Dried red chillies, crumbled • 3 tbs Torn basil leaves • Extra virgin olive oil

Lightly beat the ricotta. Add half the lemon juice and all the zest, season with salt, pepper and the chillies and stir in 4 tbs of olive oil.

Cook the langoustines in boiling salted water for 2 minutes, then drain. Cool enough to peel off the shells. Cut each langoustine in half lengthways, put in a bowl and season whilst warm. Drizzle with a little olive oil and add the rest of the lemon juice.

Cook the tagliatelle in boiling salted water until al dente. Drain, keeping back 3 tbs of the cooking water. Add the tagliatelle to the ricotta, adding the cooking water to loosen. Toss to coat each ribbon, then stir in the basil, langoustines and their juices. Serve with the lemon quarters.

Tagliatelle with langoustines and ricotta (Recipe 69)

70 Taglierini with clams and fried zucchini

350g Taglierini • 1.5kg Clams, scrubbed • 500g Zucchini, finely sliced into discs • 2 Garlic cloves, peeled and finely chopped • 1 Dried red chilli, crumbled • 250ml White wine • 50g Unsalted butter • 3 tbs Chopped flat-leaf parsley • 1 Lemon, cut into quarters • Extra virgin olive oil

Discard any open clams that do not close when tapped on the side of the sink.

Heat 1 tbs of olive oil in a thick-bottomed pan, add the garlic and chilli and cook for 1 minute. Add the clams and the wine, cover the pan and cook over a high heat until the clams open, about 3 minutes. Drain, reserving the liquid. Take the clams out of their shells, discarding the shells.

Return the clam liquid to the pan and boil to reduce by half. Test for seasoning. Lower the heat and stir in the butter. Remove from the heat, stir in the clams and add the parsley.

Heat 5 tbs of olive oil in a thick-bottomed frying pan and fry the zucchini in one layer at a time until lightly browned on each side. Drain on kitchen paper. Season.

Cook the taglierini in boiling salted water until al dente. Drain and add to the clam sauce. Toss together. Serve with the zucchini on top and with the lemon.

71 Spaghetti with bottarga

350g Spaghetti • 200g Bottarga, two thirds grated on the fine side of a cheese grater • Juice of 2 lemons • 2 Dried red chillies, crumbled • Extra virgin olive oil

Slowly stir the lemon juice into the grated bottarga to form a thick cream. Add 120ml olive oil, drop by drop, as you would for mayonnaise, to form a thick sauce.

Cook the spaghetti in boiling salted water until al dente. Drain, reserving 2 tbs of the cooking water. Stir the water into the bottarga sauce to loosen, then add the spaghetti. Toss together to coat each strand. Season with the chillies and a little black pepper.

Serve with the remaining bottarga grated over.

CHAPTER
FIVE
MEAT
SAUCES

72 Penne alla carbonara • 73 Penne with sausage sauce • 74 Penne alla matriciana • 75 Farfalle with prosciutto, mint and peas • 76 Rigatoni with beef, tomato and red wine • 77 Tagliatelle alla carbonara with prosciutto • 78 Tagliatelle with prosciutto, rosemary and radicchio 79 Pappardelle with hare sauce • 80 Pappardelle with roast duck • 81 Pappardelle with tomato, pancetta, white wine and cream • 82 Conchiglie with asparagus and prosciutto • 83 Spaghetti with parsley and pancetta • 84 Penne with sausage and ricotta • 85 Taglierini with pancetta and trevise • 86 Orecchiette with broccoli 87 Spaghetti with prosciutto, peas and spring onions 88 Tagliatelle with pancetta and borlotti

72 Penne alla carbonara

*350g Penne • 200g Pancetta, cut into matchsticks •
6 Egg yolks • 120ml Double cream • 100g Parmesan,
freshly grated • Extra virgin olive oil*

Heat 2 tbs of olive oil in a pan and fry the pancetta,
allowing its fat to release into the oil. Fry until the
pancetta becomes crisp. Add black pepper and keep
warm.

Beat the egg yolks into the cream, season, and stir in
half the Parmesan.

Cook the penne in boiling salted water until al dente.
Drain, stir into the pancetta and toss to combine.
Immediately add the egg mixture, letting the heat of
the pasta cook the egg. Stir to combine. Add the
remaining Parmesan and serve.

73 Penne with sausage sauce

*350g Penne • 6 Fresh Italian pork sausages, skins
removed, sausage meat crumbled • 2 Red onions,
peeled and chopped • 4 Garlic cloves, peeled and
finely chopped • 2 Dried red chillies, crumbled •
2 Fresh bay leaves • 150ml Red wine • 2 x 400g Tins
of peeled plum tomatoes, drained of their juices •
1/2 Nutmeg, freshly grated • 150ml Double cream •
100g Parmesan, freshly grated • Extra virgin olive oil*

Heat 2 tbs of olive oil in a thick-bottomed pan. Add the sausage meat and fry, stirring and breaking up the pieces, until lightly browned. Add the onions, garlic, chillies and bay and cook over a medium heat for 30 minutes, until the onions are brown. Pour in the wine and stir, scraping up all the sausage bits, until the wine evaporates. Then add the tomatoes, lower the heat, season and simmer gently for 45-60 minutes, until you have a thick, dark sauce. Stir in the nutmeg, cream and half the Parmesan.

Cook the penne in boiling salted water until al dente. Drain and mix into the sauce. Toss together and serve with the remaining Parmesan over.

74 Penne alla matriciana

*350g Penne • 200g Pancetta, cut into fine matchsticks
• 2 Dried red chillies, crumbled • 2 tbs Rosemary •
2 Red onions, peeled and finely chopped • 150ml Red
wine • 2 x 400g Tins of peeled plum tomatoes,
drained of their juices • 100g Parmesan, freshly grated
• Extra virgin olive oil*

Heat 2 tbs of olive oil in a thick-bottomed pan, add
the pancetta and fry slowly, allowing its fat to release
into the oil. Continue to cook until the pancetta
becomes crisp. Add the chillies, rosemary and onions
to the pan and cook until the onions become brown
and caramelised. This will take 15-20 minutes.

Add the wine, let it be absorbed by the onions, then
add the tomatoes. Break the tomatoes up by stirring.
Season, then turn the heat to low and simmer for 30
minutes, until you have a thick sauce.

Cook the penne in boiling salted water until al dente.
Drain and add to the sauce. Toss well and serve with
the Parmesan.

75 Farfalle with prosciutto, mint and peas

350g Farfalle • 8 Prosciutto slices, 4 kept whole, 4 torn into pieces • 2 tbs Mint leaves • 500g Peas (podded weight) • 100g Unsalted butter • 200g Large spring onions, peeled and sliced • 150ml Double cream • 50g Parmesan, freshly grated

Heat half the butter in a thick-bottomed saucepan, add the spring onions and cook until soft and beginning to colour. Chop half the mint and add to the pan with the peas. Pour over enough water just to cover the peas and place a layer of the whole prosciutto slices on top. Simmer very gently for 10 minutes or until the peas are soft. Add more water if the level goes below that of the peas.

Put half the peas and prosciutto into a food processor with the remaining mint and pulse-chop to a rough texture. Return this to the pan and combine the 2 different-textured sauces. Add the cream, bring to the boil and test for seasoning.

Cook the farfalle in boiling salted water until al dente. Drain, retaining 3 tbs of the pasta water, and add to the sauce. Toss to combine, adding the reserved water if the sauce is too thick.

Serve with the pieces of torn prosciutto over each plate and the Parmesan sprinkled over.

Farfalle with prosciutto, mint and peas (Recipe 75)

76 Rigatoni with beef, tomato and red wine

350g Rigatoni • 250g Beef fillet, trimmed • 1 ½ x 400g Tins of peeled plum tomatoes, drained of their juices • 350ml Red wine • 100g Unsalted butter • 4 Garlic cloves, peeled and finely chopped • 1 tbs Ground black pepper • 75g Parmesan, freshly grated • Extra virgin olive oil

Cut the beef fillet across into slices 5mm thick, then cut it into 1cm strips. Heat the butter in a thick-bottomed pan, add the garlic and fry gently until brown. Add the tomatoes and season. Cook over a medium heat for 10 minutes, stirring to break up the tomatoes, then add half the wine. Continue to cook quite fast, adding the remaining wine as the sauce reduces. Cook for a total of 30 minutes, using up all the wine. Stir in the black pepper.

Heat 2 tbs of olive oil in a flat, thick-bottomed pan until very hot. Add the beef pieces and season. Fry very briefly, just to brown each piece on both sides. Add the tomato to the pan and stir to combine the sauce.

Cook the rigatoni in boiling salted water until al dente. Drain and add to the sauce. Serve with the Parmesan sprinkled over.

77 Tagliatelle alla carbonara with prosciutto

350g Dried egg tagliatelle • 300g Prosciutto slices, cut into strips 1cm wide • 100g Unsalted butter • 150ml White wine • 6 Egg yolks • 50g Parmesan, freshly grated, plus extra for serving • 50g Aged pecorino, freshly grated • Extra virgin olive oil

Heat 1 tbs of olive oil in a thick-bottomed pan, add two thirds of the prosciutto and fry very briefly. Add half the butter and the wine. Simmer for 2-3 minutes, just to combine the wine with the butter and the prosciutto juices.

Mix the egg yolks with the cheeses and season. Cook the tagliatelle in boiling salted water until al dente, then drain, reserving a few tablespoons of the pasta water. Add the pasta to the prosciutto, then stir in the egg mixture, letting the heat of the pasta cook the egg. Add the reserved cooking water if the sauce seems too thick. Stir in the remaining prosciutto and serve with the extra Parmesan.

Tagliatelle alla carbonara with prosciutto (Recipe 77)

78 Tagliatelle with prosciutto, rosemary and radicchio

350g Dried egg tagliatelle • 300g Prosciutto slices, cut into strips 1cm wide • 2 tbs Rosemary leaves, chopped seconds before using • 1 Radicchio head, outside leaves discarded, cut into ribbons 1cm wide • 125g Unsalted butter • 1 Garlic clove, peeled and finely sliced • 50g Parmesan, freshly grated

Melt half the butter in a thick-bottomed pan. Add the garlic and rosemary and cook for 2 minutes to soften the garlic and infuse the rosemary. Add half the radicchio and prosciutto. Cook just to wilt the radicchio, then season and keep warm.

Cook the tagliatelle in boiling salted water until al dente. Drain and add to the radicchio. Add the rest of the butter and half the Parmesan. Toss to coat the pasta, then add the remaining raw prosciutto and radicchio. Mix well and serve with the remaining Parmesan.

79 Pappardelle with hare sauce

350g Pappardelle • 1 Small hare, jointed into pieces of saddle and legs • Flour for dusting • 2 Red onions, peeled and chopped • 1 Celery heart, chopped • 2 Carrots, finely chopped • 3 Garlic cloves, peeled and finely chopped • 1 Cinnamon stick, crumbled • 3 Cloves, crushed • 500ml Red wine • 1 x 400g Tin of peeled plum tomatoes • 100g Parmesan, freshly

grated, plus extra for serving • 3 tbs Double cream •
Extra virgin olive oil

Heat 3 tbs of olive oil in a wide, thick-bottomed pan. Season the hare pieces and dust with flour. Add the hare to the pan and fry in the hot oil until evenly browned. Remove from the pan to a bowl. Add 2 tbs of olive oil to the pan, lower the heat and add the onions, celery and carrots, stirring to scrape up the bits. Cook for 15 minutes or until soft. Add the garlic, cinnamon and cloves, then season. Cook for 5 minutes, then pour in the wine and add the hare and any juices from the bowl. Finally add the tomatoes. Turn the heat to low, cover and simmer for 1 hour. Pick out the saddle pieces, as they will be cooked, leaving the legs to cook for a further 30 minutes. If the sauce becomes too dry, add enough boiling water to loosen it.

Remove all the hare from the sauce and allow to cool, then take all the meat off the bones. Chop the saddle meat and set aside. Roughly chop the leg meat and return it to the sauce. Remove the cloves and cinnamon. Briefly pulse-chop the leg meat and sauce in a food processor.

Heat this sauce in a thick-bottomed pan, add the saddle meat, Parmesan and cream and stir together for 2 minutes. Season.

Cook the pappardelle in boiling salted water until al dente. Drain and stir into the sauce. Serve with the Parmesan sprinkled over.

80   Pappardelle with roast duck

350g Dried egg pappardelle • 1 Small Gressingham duck • 10 Sage leaves • 5 Garlic cloves, peeled • 1 tbs Juniper berries, crushed • 2 Carrots, halved lengthways • 1 Head of celery, cut into quarters lengthways • 1 Red onion, peeled and sliced • 1 x 400g Tin of peeled plum tomatoes, drained of their juices • 1 Cinnamon stick, broken into pieces • 2 Dried red chillies, crumbled • 400ml Red wine • 100ml Double cream • 100g Parmesan, freshly grated • Extra virgin olive oil

Preheat the oven to 200°C/Gas Mark 6.

Pull out the extra lumps of fat from inside the duck. Prick the fatty area around the tops of the legs with a cooking fork. Season the duck inside and out with lots of sea salt and black pepper. Place half the sage leaves and 2 of the garlic cloves in the cavity with the juniper berries.

Heat 2 tbs of olive oil in a large casserole. Brown the duck on all sides and remove to a bowl. Add the carrots, celery, onion and remaining garlic cloves to the pan and brown lightly. Add the remaining sage, plus the tomatoes, cinnamon and chillies, stir to combine, then return the duck, breast-side up, to the pan. Pour in the wine and bring to the boil. Place the casserole in the preheated oven and roast for 45 minutes.

Turn the duck over and continue to roast for 30 minutes, or until the flesh falls from the bone on the leg. Remove the duck from the pan and allow to cool. Then pull off all the flesh, discarding fatty bits and any skin that is not crisp. Chop the meat finely, or pulse-chop in a food processor. Pass the vegetables and the juices from the casserole through a mouli. Mix this with the chopped duck. Put in a saucepan, add the cream and, when hot, stir in half the Parmesan. Season.

Cook the pappardelle in boiling salted water until al dente. Drain and add to the sauce. Toss to combine and serve with the remaining Parmesan.

81 Pappardelle with tomato, pancetta, white wine and cream

350g Dried egg pappardelle • 6 Plum tomatoes, skinned and roughly chopped • 150g Pancetta, sliced and cut into 2cm pieces • 120ml White wine • 120ml Double cream • 150g Unsalted butter • 2 Dried red chillies, crumbled • ½ tbs Freshly ground black pepper • 100g Parmesan, freshly grated

Melt the butter in a thick-bottomed pan, add the pancetta and cook over a low heat, stirring occasionally, for 20 minutes to allow the flavours of the pancetta to combine with the butter. Eventually the pancetta will become crisp. Add the chillies, black pepper and then the white wine. Cook for 5 minutes to reduce the wine, then add the tomatoes and some sea salt and simmer for 15 minutes. Add the cream and cook for a further 15 minutes, or until the sauce thickens.

Cook the pappardelle in boiling salted water until al dente. Drain and stir into the sauce. Stir in half the Parmesan. Serve with the remaining Parmesan over.

82 Conchiglie with asparagus and prosciutto

350g Conchiglie • 750g Asparagus, tough ends snapped off, tender stems and tips thinly sliced • 250g Prosciutto slices, cut into strips 1cm wide • 1kg Peas, podded • 50g Unsalted butter • 200ml Double cream • 150ml Chicken stock (made from 1 stock cube) • 2 tbs Mint leaves, roughly chopped just before using • 50g Parmesan, freshly grated, plus extra for serving

Cook the peas in boiling salted water for 2 minutes, remove with a slotted spoon and put in a bowl with half the butter. Cook the asparagus in the same water for 2-3 minutes, until al dente. Drain and add to the peas. Mix and keep warm.

Heat the remaining butter in a thick-bottomed pan and add the prosciutto. Fry briefly, just until it softens and becomes translucent. Add the peas and asparagus and remove from the heat.

Heat the cream and stock together in a small saucepan until boiling, then turn the heat down and season. Cook gently for 10-15 minutes to reduce by a third. Pour into the asparagus mixture.

Cook the conchiglie in boiling salted water until al dente. Drain, keeping back 2-3 tbs of the pasta water. Add the pasta to the sauce with the chopped mint and Parmesan. Stir in the retained pasta water if the sauce is too thick. Toss well and serve with the extra Parmesan.

83 Spaghetti with parsley and pancetta

*350g Spaghetti • 4 tbs Chopped flat-leaf parsley •
300g Pancetta, finely sliced • 100g Unsalted butter •
1 Red onion, peeled and finely chopped • 2 Garlic
cloves, peeled and finely chopped • 1 Dried red chilli,
crumbled • 120g Parmesan, freshly grated • Extra
virgin olive oil*

Set aside 4 pancetta slices and cut the rest into
matchsticks.

Heat the butter in a medium, thick-bottomed pan.
Add the onion and cook over a medium heat until
light brown. Add the chopped pancetta and garlic and
cook, stirring, for 5 minutes. Season and add the chilli.
Stir in the parsley, cook just to wilt and remove from
the heat.

Heat a small pan, brush with olive oil and fry the
pancetta slices in it to crisp them. Drain on kitchen
paper.

Cook the spaghetti in boiling salted water until al
dente. Drain, keeping back 2-3 tbs of the pasta water.
Add the spaghetti to the parsley mixture, stir in half
the Parmesan and add the reserved pasta water if the
sauce seems too thick. Serve with the crisp pancetta
and the remaining Parmesan.

84   Penne with sausage and ricotta

*350g Penne • 4 Fresh Italian sausages • 100g
Ricotta • 1 Red onion, peeled and chopped • 1 Fennel
bulb, chopped • 3 Garlic cloves, peeled and finely
chopped • 150ml Red wine • 2 x 400g Tins of peeled
plum tomatoes, drained of their juices, then roughly
chopped in the tin • 3 tbs Basil leaves • 50g
Parmesan, freshly grated • Extra virgin olive oil*

Put the sausages in a small pan and just cover with
water. Bring to the boil, then simmer until all the
water has evaporated and the sausages are cooked;
the pan will become oily. Remove the sausages, cool,
then remove the meat from the casings. Crumble the
meat with your fingers.

Heat 1 tbs of oil in the pan you cooked the sausages
in. Add the onion and fennel and cook until soft and
beginning to brown. Add the garlic and cook for half
a minute. Add the sausage meat, wine and tomatoes
and bring to the boil. Simmer for 20 minutes and
season.

Cook the penne in boiling salted water until al dente.
Drain and add to the sauce. Add the basil and stir.

Beat the ricotta with a fork and season. Place 1 tbs of
ricotta on each plate. Spoon the pasta over the
ricotta, but do not combine. Serve with the Parmesan.

Penne with sausage and ricotta (Recipe 84)

85 Orecchiette with broccoli

350g Orecchiette • 500g Broccoli, cut into small florets • 150g Pancetta slices, cut into matchsticks • 2 Garlic cloves, peeled and finely sliced • 1 tsp Fennel seeds, crushed • 3 Dried red chillies, crumbled • 50g Parmesan, freshly grated • Extra virgin olive oil

Cook the broccoli in boiling salted water until soft, then drain.

Heat 2 tbs of olive oil in a thick-bottomed pan, add the pancetta, garlic and fennel seeds and cook gently until soft, not crisp. Add the broccoli and chillies and season. Mix together over a gentle heat for 2-3 minutes to combine the flavours.

Cook the orecchiette in boiling salted water until al dente. Drain and add to the sauce. Mix together well and serve with the Parmesan.

86 Taglierini with pancetta and trevise

350g Taglierini • 200g Pancetta, sliced, then cut into fine matchsticks • 500g Trevise or radicchio, trimmed and finely sliced across • 70g Unsalted butter • 2 Red onions, peeled and finely sliced • 2 Garlic cloves, peeled and finely sliced • 2 Dried red chillies, crumbled • 2 tbs Chopped thyme • 100ml White wine • 120ml Chicken stock (made with 1 cube) •

*50g Parmesan, freshly grated, plus extra for serving •
Extra virgin olive oil*

Heat the butter with 1 tbs of olive oil in a large, thick-bottomed pan. Add the pancetta and cook until it releases its fat and becomes lightly crisp. Add the onions, garlic and chillies and cook until the onions are tender. Add 1 more tbs of olive oil, then add the trevise and thyme. Stir and cook for 1-2 minutes or until the trevise wilts. Add the white wine and stock and bring to the boil. Turn the heat down and simmer for 20 minutes to reduce the liquid. Season.

Cook the taglierini in boiling salted water until al dente. Drain and add to the sauce, along with the Parmesan. Toss together. Serve with extra Parmesan.

87 Spaghetti with prosciutto, peas and spring onions

350g Spaghetti • 150g Prosciutto slices, torn into small pieces • 400g Podded peas • 200g Spring onions, white part only, chopped • 100g Unsalted butter • 1 Garlic clove, peeled and finely chopped • 2 tbs Chopped flat-leaf parsley • 50g Parmesan, freshly grated • Extra virgin olive oil

Heat the butter in a wide, thick-bottomed pan. Add the spring onions and soften gently, then add the peas, some salt and 3 tbs of hot water. Simmer gently until the water evaporates. Add the garlic and parsley and 3 tbs of olive oil. Cover and cook on a low heat for 15 minutes. Add the prosciutto. If more liquid is needed, add olive oil, not water. Cook until the peas are dark and soft.

Cook the spaghetti in boiling salted water until al dente. Drain and add to the peas. Stir to mix together and serve with the Parmesan.

88 Tagliatelle with pancetta and borlotti

350g Dried egg tagliatelle • 150g Pancetta slices, cut into 1cm pieces • 500g Cooked borlotti beans, drained of their juices • 1 Red onion, peeled and chopped • 2 Garlic cloves, peeled and finely sliced • 1 x 400g Tin of peeled plum tomatoes, drained of their juices • 100ml Double cream • 3 tbs Torn basil leaves • 50g Parmesan, freshly grated • Extra virgin olive oil

Heat 2 tbs of olive oil in a thick-bottomed pan. Add the onion and cook until soft, then add the garlic and pancetta and cook until the pancetta is translucent, about 10 minutes. Add the tomatoes, chopping them up to make a sauce, and cook for a further 10 minutes. Season, then stir in the borlotti beans and cream. Cook for 5-10 minutes, until the sauce is thick. Add the basil and 2 tbs of olive oil.

Cook the tagliatelle in boiling salted water until al dente. Drain, retaining 3-4 tbs of the pasta water. Add the tagliatelle to the beans, adding the retained pasta water if the sauce is too thick. Toss together, drizzle with olive oil and serve with the Parmesan.

Tagliatelle with pancetta and borlotti (Recipe 88)

CHAPTER
SIX
STUFFED
PASTA

89 Fresh pasta • 90 Spinach pasta • 91 Pasta
pieces with tomatoes and black olives • 92 Silk
handkerchiefs with green beans and pesto
93 Ravioli with potato and rocket • 94 Ravioli verdi
with ricotta • 95 Ravioli with pumpkin, mascarpone
and sage butter • 96 Agnoli with roast pork
97 Rotolo stuffed with spinach

89 Fresh pasta

500g Tipo 00 flour • 4 Medium eggs • 6 Medium egg yolks • 1 tsp Maldon sea salt • 50g Semolina flour, for dusting

Use an electric mixer fitted with a dough hook. Sift the flour into the mixer bowl. Add the eggs, yolks and salt to the centre. Knead slowly, allowing the mixture to come together. Keep on the lowest speed for 10 minutes or until the ball of dough is smooth.

Dust your work surface with semolina flour. Divide the dough in half and knead each half by hand for 3-4 minutes, until soft and velvety. Wrap each piece in cling film and put in the fridge for 1 hour.

To make the pasta into sheets it is best to use a pasta machine. Dust the surface around the machine with semolina flour. Cut each dough ball in half. Keep the pieces you are not immediately rolling out wrapped in cling film. Set the rollers on the widest setting, usually 10. Pass the first ball of dough through to form a thick sheet, fold the sheet into 3 to form a thick, short piece, then turn it around and put it through again. After 10 such folds, the pasta should feel silky. Only then reduce the settings on the machine, one by one, passing the dough through each time to form a longer, thinner sheet, until you reach the thinness required. Cut the sheets in half if they become too long to manage.

If rolling the pasta by hand, hand-knead and hand-roll the dough the equivalent of 10 times through the machine. Do this in a cool place so the pasta does not become too dry before you cut it into shape.

---

90 Spinach pasta

700g Tipo 00 flour • 2 Medium eggs • 9 Medium egg yolks • 2 Egg-sized balls of blanched spinach, squeezed dry and finely chopped (you will need about 500g fresh spinach) • 1 tsp Maldon sea salt• Semolina flour for dusting

Using an electric mixer fitted with a dough hook, combine the flour with the eggs, yolks and spinach. Add the salt. Knead the dough on a low speed as for Fresh Pasta, above. If the dough seems too wet or sticky, add a little more flour.

Hand-knead the dough on a floured surface until smooth. Wrap in cling film and place in the fridge for 1 hour.

Roll out as described in Fresh Pasta, above.

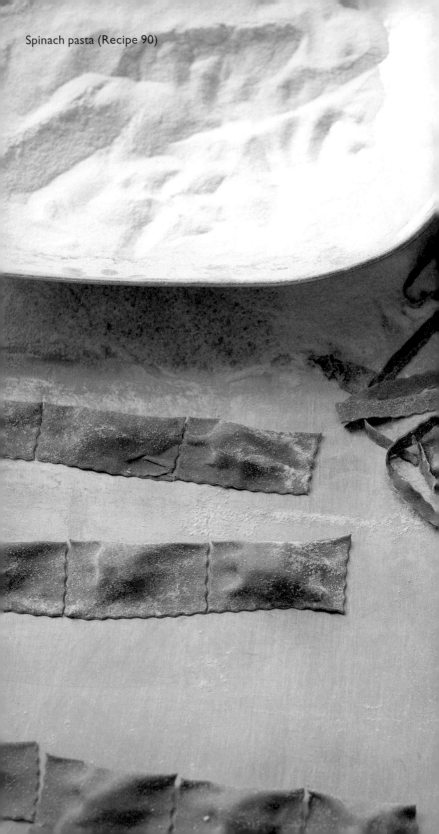

Spinach pasta (Recipe 90)

91 Pasta pieces with tomatoes and black olives

1 quantity of Fresh Pasta (Recipe 89), rolled out on a medium setting and cut into 4cm squares • 1kg Cherry tomatoes, halved and squeezed to remove juice and seeds • 1 x 400g Tin of peeled plum tomatoes, drained of their juices, then chopped roughly • 60g Small black olives preserved in brine, stoned • 2 Garlic cloves, peeled and finely chopped • 2 tbs Basil leaves • 50g Pecorino, freshly grated (hard aged pecorino is best) • Extra virgin olive oil

Heat 2 tbs of olive oil in a thick-bottomed pan and add the garlic. Cook briefly to colour, then add the cherry tomato halves and some salt. Cook until the tomatoes become soft, then add the tinned tomatoes, stirring them into the cherry tomatoes to form a sauce. Cook over a high heat for 5 minutes. Check for seasoning, adding pepper. Remove from the heat and add the olives and basil.

Cook the fresh pasta in boiling salted water until al dente (approximately 2 minutes, depending on thickness). Drain and add to the tomato sauce. Toss together very gently. Serve with the pecorino and a drizzle of olive oil.

92 Silk handkerchiefs with green beans and pesto

1 quantity of Fresh Pasta (Recipe 89), rolled out to the thinnest setting, then cut into 8-10cm squares • 300g Fine green beans, topped and tailed • 50g Unsalted butter • 50g Parmesan, freshly grated • Extra virgin olive oil

Pesto
1 Garlic clove, peeled • 3 tbs Basil leaves • 1 tsp Maldon salt • 25g Pecorino Romano, freshly grated • 25g Parmesan, freshly grated • 10g Pine nuts, smashed to a paste• Extra virgin olive oil

To make the pesto, use a stick blender with a sharp blade. Place the garlic, basil leaves and Maldon salt in a bowl and chop to a pulp. Add 100ml olive oil and blend until you have a loose sauce. Stir in the cheeses and pine nuts.

Cook the green beans in boiling salted water until tender. Drain, retaining 3 tbs of the water. Return the beans to the pan with the retained water and add the butter. Stir 1 tbs of pesto into the beans and keep warm.

Cook the handkerchiefs a few at a time in boiling salted water until al dente, about 2 minutes. Remove with a slotted spoon. To serve, spread a small amount of pesto onto each warm plate, arrange 3 or 4 sheets of pasta on top, cover with some beans and another small amount of pesto on top. Drizzle with olive oil and serve with the Parmesan.

93 Ravioli with potato and rocket

1 quantity of Fresh Pasta (Recipe 89) • Flour for dusting • 50g Pecorino, freshly grated • 3 tbs Rocket leaves, plus a few leaves for serving, roughly chopped • 1 Fresh red chilli, cut in half lengthways, de-seeded and very thinly sliced • Extra virgin olive oil

Filling
1kg Floury potatoes, washed but not peeled • 100g Rocket, finely chopped • 2 Garlic cloves, peeled and finely sliced • 1 Dried red chilli, crumbled • 1 tbs Fennel seeds, crushed • 50g Pecorino, freshly grated • Extra virgin olive oil

To make the filling, cook the potatoes in boiling salted water until soft. Drain and cool. Scrape off the skins and pass the flesh through a coarse mouli. Season.

Heat 2 tbs of olive oil in a thick-bottomed pan, add the garlic and fry until soft. Add the chilli and fennel seeds. Stir in three-quarters of the rocket, cover and remove from the heat. Mix the cooked rocket and the remaining raw rocket with the potato. Add the pecorino and check for seasoning.

Divide the pasta into small balls and keep wrapped in cling film, except for the one you are rolling out. Dust the surface around your pasta machine with semolina flour. Roll out the pasta into long sheets on the thinnest setting. Place teaspoonfuls of the filling on the pasta sheet, 6cm apart. Lightly brush around the filling with a brush dipped in water, then fold over the pasta sheet, press round each filling to seal and cut out the ravioli. You will be cutting around 3 sides of each one, the fourth side being the fold. Dust a large tray with flour and place the ravioli on it as you make them. Do not let them touch each other.

Cook the ravioli in boiling salted water for about 4 minutes. Test where the pasta is thickest. Drain and serve with a drizzle of olive oil, the pecorino and a scattering of fresh rocket.

94 Ravioli verdi with ricotta

1 quantity of Spinach Pasta (Recipe 89) • Flour for dusting • 100g Unsalted butter, softened • Parmesan, freshly grated, for serving

Filling
500g Ricotta • 2 tbs Chopped basil • 2 tbs Chopped marjoram • 2 tbs Chopped flat-leaf parsley • 1/4 Nutmeg, freshly grated • 60g Parmesan, freshly grated

To make the filling, beat the ricotta with a fork, add the nutmeg, herbs and Parmesan and season. Mix and test for flavour. Add more herbs or ricotta if necessary. You should have a thick, pale green paste.

Roll out the pasta as described in Recipe 93, arrange the filling on it as before, and cut into ravioli about 4cm square. Place on a tray dusted with flour. Cook the ravioli in batches in boiling salted water until al dente, about 4 minutes. Remove with a slotted spoon and place in a warm serving dish with the softened butter. Serve with the Parmesan.

95 Ravioli with pumpkin, mascarpone and sage butter

1 quantity of Fresh Pasta (Recipe 89) • Semolina flour for dusting • 50g Parmesan, freshly grated

Filling
500g Pumpkin (or onion squash or butternut squash), peeled, seeded and cut into 3cm cubes • 250g Mascarpone • 50g Unsalted butter • 1 Potato (about 200g), peeled and cut into 4 pieces • 3 Garlic cloves, peeled • 1 Fresh red chilli • 100g Parmesan, freshly grated

Sage butter
16 Sage leaves • 120g Unsalted butter • ½ tsp Maldon salt

To make the filling, heat the butter in a thick-bottomed pan and add the pumpkin, potato, garlic and whole chilli. Stir and fry for 3 minutes, then add 100ml boiling water. Season. Cover the pan, turn the heat down and cook until the vegetables are tender and all the liquid has been absorbed, about 20 minutes. Remove from the heat and take out the chilli. Cut it in half, scrape out the flesh, discard the skin and seeds, then add the flesh back to the pumpkin. When cool, smash the pumpkin in a bowl until well mashed. Add the mascarpone and Parmesan and test for seasoning. The mixture should be thick enough to spoon out on to your pasta sheets. Make the ravioli as described in Recipe 93.

To make the sage butter, gently soften the butter in a small pan, then add the sage leaves and Maldon salt. On a very low heat, soften the sage leaves into the butter, keeping the butter as thick as possible.

Cook the ravioli in boiling salted water until al dente. Serve with the sage butter and the Parmesan.

96 Agnoli with roast pork

1 quantity of Fresh Pasta (Recipe 89) • 100g Semolina flour for dusting • 50g Unsalted butter • 50g Parmesan, freshly grated

Filling
2.5kg Pork loin on the bone • 4 Rosemary branches, washed • 15 Garlic cloves, peeled, kept whole • 1 Bottle of chardonnay • 100g Unsalted butter • 150g Parmesan, freshly grated

Preheat the oven to 220°/Gas Mark 7.

Season the meat generously with sea salt and black pepper. Place the pork loin, fat side up, in a roasting tray and roast for 15 minutes. Reduce the oven to 175°C/Gas Mark 4, add the garlic cloves and rosemary, placing the pork loin on top. Pour in half the chardonnay and roast for 1–1½ hours or until cooked. During roasting, add more wine if there is no juice in the pan. Add the remaining wine and the butter, stir to combine to make a small amount of sauce. Remove the pork from the oven and allow to cool in the pan. Pull the meat from the bones and »

« cut off any excess fat from the back. Finely chop the meat or put through a mincer and put into a large bowl. Drain the pan juices and add to the meat. Add the cooked garlic and mix well. Add the Parmesan and check the seasoning. The mixture should not be wet. Using a spoon, form the mixture into small cherry-sized balls – you should get 24 balls from this mixture.

Roll out the pasta to the thinnest setting. Cut the sheets into 24 5x5cm squares, place a ball in the centre of each and spray lightly with water. Pull together 2 opposite corners and pinch together above the filling, then push the other two corners in towards the already joined corners and pinch the edges to form a little pasta parcel. Dust with semolina. Keep in the fridge if not using straight away.

Cook the agnoli in boiling salted water in batches. Keep in a warm bowl with a little melted butter. Serve with sage butter (see Recipe 95) and the Parmesan.

97   Rotolo stuffed with spinach

1 quantity of Fresh Pasta (Recipe 89) • Sage Butter (Recipe 95) • Semolina flour for dusting • 50g Parmesan, freshly grated

Filling
500g Spinach, cooked and squeezed dry • 30g Dried porcini mushrooms, soaked in 100ml boiling water for 15 minutes • 1 Garlic clove, peeled and chopped • 150g Unsalted butter • 250g Ricotta • 50g Parmesan, freshly grated • ½ Nutmeg, freshly grated • Extra virgin olive oil

To make the filling, drain the porcini, reserving the soaking liquid. Rinse the porcini in a sieve under a running tap to remove any grit. Strain the soaking liquid through a sieve lined with kitchen paper.

Heat 2 tbs of olive oil in a small pan, add the garlic and soften, then add the porcini and 50g of the butter. Cook gently for 15 minutes or until soft, adding a little of the porcini liquid to keep it moist. Season. Remove from the heat and chop finely.

Mix the ricotta with a fork, then season. Chop the spinach finely, then stir it into the ricotta. Add the Parmesan and nutmeg.

Roll out the pasta as thinly as you can into 20cm lengths. Join the lengths to form a rough square, brushing the long edges with water to seal. Make 2 squares. Spoon the mushroom mixture along the pasta edge closest to you. Cover the rest of the pasta with the ricotta mixture in a layer about 1cm thick. »

Rotolo stuffed with spinach (Recipe 97)

CHAPTER SEVEN
GNOCCHI & GNUDI

98 Gnocchi romani • 99 Pumpkin gnocchi • 100 Potato gnocchi • 101 Gnocchi with prosciutto 102 Gnocchi with tomato sauce • 103 Spinach gnocchi • 104 Gnudi bianchi • 105 Gnudi verdi

98 Gnocchi romani

*1 litre Milk • 200g Semolina flour • 3 Egg yolks •
120g Parmesan, freshly grated, plus extra for serving •
150g Unsalted butter • ¼ Nutmeg, freshly grated •
30g White truffle (optional), brushed clean*

Bring the milk to the boil in a medium, thick-bottomed saucepan. Lower the heat to a simmer and slowly whisk in the semolina flour. Cook, stirring, for 15 minutes. Remove from the heat, cool for 5 minutes, then stir in the egg yolks one by one, followed by 100g Parmesan and 100g butter. Add the nutmeg and season. Mix well together. Moisten a tray with cold water and turn the gnocchi mixture onto it. Spread to a thickness of 1.5cm. When cool and firm, cut the gnocchi using a champagne flute or a biscuit cutter of the same diameter, dipped in cold water. Place the gnocchi on baking parchment and refrigerate for 1 hour.

Preheat the oven to 200°C/Gas Mark 6.

Butter an ovenproof oval china dish and scatter a little Parmesan over. Place the gnocchi in the dish, overlapping each one slightly with the next. Dot with the remaining butter, sprinkle with the remaining Parmesan and bake in the preheated oven for 15 minutes, or until the gnocchi puff up and a light crust has formed on top. Serve hot with extra Parmesan and, if you have one, white truffle shaved over each serving.

99   Pumpkin gnocchi

1kg Onion squash, skin scrubbed clean • 2 Dried red chillies, crumbled • 2 tsp Dried oregano • 750g Desiree potatoes • 3 Eggs, beaten • 100g Semolina flour • ½ Nutmeg, freshly grated • Polenta flour, for dusting • Plain flour, for dusting • 60g Butter, softened • Sage Butter (see Recipe 95) • 50g Parmesan, freshly grated • Extra virgin olive oil

Preheat the oven to 190°C/Gas Mark 5.

Cut the squash in half, scoop out the seeds, then cut into slices 3cm thick. Season, and sprinkle with the chillies and oregano. Put the slices on a baking tray drizzled with olive oil and bake for 35 minutes or until soft. Keep warm.

Cook the potatoes in their skins in boiling salted water until tender. Drain, then peel while still hot.

Pass the squash and potato through a mouli whilst hot. Add the eggs, one by one, stirring to combine, then sift in the semolina flour. Add the nutmeg and season. Beat the mixture to form a stiff dough.

Dust a work surface with polenta and plain flour. Divide the dough into 4. Pull out each piece into a sausage 2cm thick and cut it into 3cm lengths. Form into gnocchi by lightly rolling each piece over the back of a fork.

Cook the gnocchi in batches in boiling salted water. They will come to the surface after 2-3 minutes; continue to cook for 2-3 minutes more. Test for doneness. Remove with a slotted spoon and place in a bowl with the softened butter. Serve with the Sage Butter (see Recipe 95) and the Parmesan.

100 Potato gnocchi

1kg Desiree potatoes, scrubbed clean • 250g Plain flour • 80g Unsalted butter • 100g Parmesan, freshly grated

Cook the potatoes in their skins in boiling salted water until soft. Drain and peel off the skin whilst hot. Immediately pass through a mouli onto a clean surface.

Sift over the flour, season and combine rapidly to form a light dough. Cut the dough into 4. Roll out into sausages 1.5cm thick, then cut into 2-3cm lengths. To form the gnocchi, press each piece against the prongs of a fork to form little ridges. These will help hold the sauce.

Cook the gnocchi in boiling salted water; they will rise to the surface in 2-3 minutes. Cook on for 30 seconds, then test for doneness. Remove with a slotted spoon to a warm dish with the butter. Toss gently to coat each gnocchi. Season and serve with the Parmesan.

101 Gnocchi with prosciutto

*1 quantity of Potato Gnocchi (Recipe 100) •
4 Prosciutto slices, each torn into 3 pieces • 300g
Swiss chard leaves, stalks removed • 1 Garlic clove,
peeled and finely sliced • Parmesan, freshly grated,
for serving • Extra virgin olive oil*

Cook the chard in boiling salted water. Drain, leave
to cool, then chop roughly.

Heat 2 tbs of olive oil in a thick-bottomed pan and
fry the garlic in it until soft. Add the chard and season.
Cook for 1 minute to combine the flavours. Keep
warm.

Cook the gnocchi as before, omitting the butter. Place
the chard in a warm serving dish, add the gnocchi and
mix together. Place the prosciutto over and drizzle
with olive oil. Serve with Parmesan.

102 Gnocchi with tomato sauce

*1 quantity of Potato Gnocchi (Recipe 100) • 2 x 400g
Tins of peeled plum tomatoes, drained of half their
juices • 2 Red onions, peeled and finely sliced •
2 Garlic cloves, peeled and finely sliced • 3 tbs Basil
leaves • 50g Parmesan, freshly grated • Extra virgin
olive oil*

Heat 2 tbs of olive oil in a thick-bottomed frying pan.
Add the onions and cook over a low heat until soft

and translucent. Add the garlic and continue to cook until the onions begin to colour. Add the tomatoes, stir to break them up, then season. Cook slowly on a moderate heat, stirring occasionally, for 45 minutes or until the tomatoes have become a thick sauce. Remove from the heat and stir in the basil. Keep warm.

Cook the gnocchi as before, omitting the butter. Drain and mix with the tomato sauce. Drizzle with olive oil and serve with the Parmesan.

103 Spinach gnocchi

500g Spinach, boiled and squeezed dry • 50g Unsalted butter, plus extra for serving • 2 tbs Marjoram leaves • 200g Ricotta • 90g Plain flour, plus extra for dusting • 3 egg yolks • 1/2 Nutmeg, freshly grated • 150g Parmesan, freshly grated, plus extra for serving

Melt the butter, add the marjoram and cook for a minute. Add the spinach and stir to combine the flavours. Season, remove from the heat and cool, then finely chop.

Beat the ricotta with a fork and sift in the flour. Add the egg yolks, nutmeg and Parmesan. Mix well together, then fold in the spinach mixture. Test for seasoning. Put the mixture in the fridge to get completely cold and firm.

Dust a tray with flour. Using 2 dessertspoons, take a spoonful of the mixture and, with the other spoon, mould it to form the gnocchi. Place the gnocchi, as

« you make them, on the tray so that they are not touching each other.

Gently cook the gnocchi in batches in boiling salted water. When they come to the surface, remove with a slotted spoon and place in a warm serving dish with a knob of butter. Keep warm whilst you cook the remainder. Serve with Sage Butter (see Recipe 95) and the extra Parmesan.

104 Gnudi bianchi

500g Ricotta • 100g Parmesan, freshly grated, plus extra for serving • 1/2 Nutmeg, freshly grated • 500g Semolina flour • 100g Unsalted butter, softened • 3 tbs Sage leaves

Beat the ricotta with a fork to lighten, then season. Add the Parmesan and nutmeg and mix until you have a thickish dough.

Cover a flat tray with half the semolina flour. Divide the dough into 4. On the tray of semolina, roll out each piece into a sausage 3.5cm thick, then cut into 2.5cm pieces. Gently form the pieces into balls, coating them as you roll them in the flour. Place on a tray thickly dusted with semolina flour.

When all the gnudi are made, add more semolina flour so they are almost submerged. Place in the fridge for 24 hours to harden.

Just before serving, put half the butter in a warm serving dish. Fry the sage leaves in the remaining butter.

Cook the gnudi in batches in boiling salted water for 3 minutes or until they rise to the surface. Remove to the serving dish with a slotted spoon. Serve with the sage butter and the extra Parmesan.

Gnudi bianchi need to be made at least 24 hours before cooking.

105 Gnudi verdi

250g Spinach, boiled and squeezed dry • 250g Ricotta • 2 Eggs • 1 Egg yolk • 100g Parmesan, freshly grated • 1/4 Nutmeg, freshly grated • 200g Semolina flour • Extra virgin olive oil

Chop the spinach finely.

Beat the ricotta with a fork, stir in the whole eggs, one by one, then the yolk. Add the spinach, Parmesan and nutmeg, mix well to form a stiff dough, and season.

Scatter a flat tray with all the semolina flour. Divide the dough into 4. On the tray of semolina, roll each piece into a sausage 2cm thick, then cut into 2cm lengths. Roll into balls, making sure they are evenly coated with the semolina.

Place in the fridge for 30 minutes to firm them up. Cook the gnudi in batches in boiling salted water for approximately 3 minutes, or until they rise to the surface. Remove with a slotted spoon, place in a warm serving dish and drizzle with olive oil.

Unlike Gnudi bianchi, Gnudi verdi can be made the day you plan to eat them as the dough contains egg.

Index

agnoli with roast pork 96
anchovies, bucatini with pangrattato
    and 55
artichokes:
    spaghetti with artichoke and parsley
        pesto 4
    tagliatelle with fresh 40
asparagus:
    conchiglie with prosciutto and 82
    linguine with clams, white asparagus
        and cinnamon 59
    penne with asparagus carbonara 24
    tagliatelle with 22
aubergines:
    farfalle with grilled aubergine and
        zucchini 47
    penne with tomato, mozzarella and 26

beef, rigatoni with tomato, red wine
    and 76
borlotti, tagliatelle with pancetta
    and 88
bottarga, spaghetti with 71
broad beans:
    linguine with 41
    taglierini with raw broad beans 12
broccoli:
    orecchiette with 86
    orecchiette with clams and 50
    orecchiette with olives and 23
bucatini:
    with anchovies and pangrattato 55
    with dried oregano 3

capers, penne with tomatoes and ricotta
    salata 1
cavolo nero, farfalle with 49
celery:
    spaghetti, boiled tomato sauce with
        carrots and 37
cheese:
    rigatoni with fontina 14
    spaghetti with pecorino 16
    tagliatelle with asparagus 22
    tagliatelle with gorgonzola 21
    taglierini with raw broad beans 12
    see also mascarpone; ricotta
chillies:
    linguine with crab, red chilli
        and extra virgin olive oil 56
    penne all'arrabbiata 25
    spaghetti with garlic, parsley,
        lemon and 45

tagliatelle with fresh figs and 46
clams:
    linguine with white asparagus,
        cinnamon and 59
    orecchiette with broccoli and 50
    spaghetti with Prosecco and 64
    spirale with prawns and 53
    taglierini with fried zucchini and 70
conchiglie:
    with asparagus and prosciutto 82
    with ricotta and rocket 17
    with tomato and dried porcini 29
crab:
    linguine with fennel and 60
    linguine with fresh red chilli, extra
        virgin olive oil and 56
crème fraîche, tagliatelle with rocket
    and 19

ditaloni, mussels and cream 52
duck:
    pappardelle with roast duck 80

eggs:
    penne alla carbonara 72
    penne with asparagus carbonara 24
    tagliatelle alla carbonara with
        prosciutto 77

farfalle:
    with cavolo nero 49
    with grilled aubergine and zucchini 47
    with prosciutto, mint and peas 75
fennel, linguine with crab and 60
figs, tagliatelle with chilli and 46
fish sauces 50–71
fresh pasta 89

garlic, spaghetti with chilli, parsley,
    lemon and 45
ginger, spaghetti with tomato and 34
gnocchi: gnocchi romani 98
    gnocchi with prosciutto 101
    gnocchi with tomato sauce 102
    potato gnocchi 100
    pumpkin gnocchi 99
    spinach gnocchi 103
gnudi bianchi 104
gnudi verdi 105
green beans:
    silk handkerchiefs with pesto and 92
    tagliatelle with 11
hare sauce, pappardelle with 79

hazelnuts:
  tagliatelle with fresh hazelnuts 8

langoustines, tagliatelle with ricotta
  and 69
leeks, pappardelle with porcini and 44
lemon:
  spaghetti with 15
  tagliatelle with cream, parsley and 20
linguine:
  with broad beans 41
  with clams, white asparagus
    and cinnamon 59
  with crab and fresh fennel 60
  with crab, red chilli and extra virgin
    olive oil 56
  with sardines 54
  with sardines and saffron 61
lobster:
  spaghetti with marinated lobster 63

mascarpone:
  ravioli with pumpkin, sage butter and
    95
  tagliatelle with fried breadcrumbs
    and 18
meat sauces 72–88
mushrooms:
  conchiglie with tomato and dried
    porcini 29
  pappardelle with leeks and porcini 44
  penne with dried porcini, tomatoes
    and cream 30
  tagliatelle with dried porcini and
    sage 42
  tagliatelle with girolle mushrooms 43
  taglierini with fresh porcini 6
mussels:
  ditaloni, mussels and cream 52
  penne with zucchini and 51
  spaghetti from Le Marche 62

olives:
  pasta pieces with tomatoes and black
    olives 91
  spaghetti with roasted red mullet
    and 66
orecchiette:
  with broccoli 86
  with broccoli and olives 23
  with clams and broccoli 50
  with scallops and rocket 57
  with tomatoes and fresh ricotta 2

oregano:
  bucatini with dried oregano 3

pancetta:
  pappardelle with tomato, white wine,
    cream and 81
  penne alla carbonara 72
  penne alla matriciana 74
  spaghetti with parsley and 83
  tagliatelle with borlotti and 88
  taglierini with trevise and 85
pappardelle:
  with hare sauce 79
  with leeks and porcini 44
  with roast duck 80
  with tomato, pancetta, white wine
    and cream 81
pasta pieces with tomatoes and
  black olives 91
peas:
  farfalle with prosciutto, mint and 75
  spaghetti with prosciutto, spring
    onions and 87
  tagliatelle with brown shrimps and 58
penne:
  penne all'arrabbiata 25
  penne alla carbonara 72
  penne alla matriciana 74
  with asparagus carbonara 24
  with aubergine, tomato
    and mozzarella 26
  with balsamic vinegar 31
  with capers, tomatoes and ricotta
    salata 1
  with deep-fried zucchini 48
  with dried porcini, tomatoes and
    cream 30
  with mussels and zucchini 51
  with sausage and ricotta 84
  with sausage sauce 73
  with tomato and nutmeg 27
  with zucchini and mint 28
  with zucchini and ricotta 13
peppers, spaghetti with tomatoes,
  capers and 35
pesto:
  spaghetti with artichoke and parsley 4
  silk handkerchiefs with green
    beans and 92
porcini see mushrooms
pork: agnoli with roast pork 96
potatoes:
  potato gnocchi 100

ravioli with rocket and 93
prawns: spaghetti in the bag 65
    spirale with clams and 53
prosciutto:
    conchiglie with asparagus and 82
    farfalle with mint, peas and 75
    gnocchi with 101
    spaghetti with peas, spring onions
        and 87
    tagliatelle alla carbonara with 77
    tagliatelle with rosemary, radicchio
        and 78
pumpkin:
    pumpkin gnocchi 99
    ravioli with mascarpone, sage butter
        and 95

radicchio, tagliatelle with prosciutto,
    rosemary and 78
ravioli:
    ravioli verdi with ricotta 94
    with potato and rocket 93
    with pumpkin, mascarpone, and
        sage butter 95
red mullet:
    spaghetti with roasted red mullet
        and olives 66
    taglierini with bay and 68
ricotta:
    conchiglie with rocket and 17
    gnudi bianchi 104
    gnudi verdi 105
    orecchiette with tomatoes and 2
    penne with sausage and 84
    penne with zucchini and 13
    ravioli verdi with 94
    rotolo stuffed with spinach 97
    spinach gnocchi 103
    tagliatelle with langoustines and 69
rigatoni:
    with beef, tomato and red wine 76
    with fontina 14
rocket:
    conchiglie with ricotta and 17
    orecchiette with scallops and 57
    ravioli with potato and 93
    tagliatelle with crème fraîche and 19
rotolo stuffed with spinach 97

sardines:
    linguine with 54
    linguine with saffron and 61

sauces:
    cheese sauces 13–22
    fish sauces 50–71
    meat sauces 72–88
    raw sauces 1–12
    vegetarian sauces 23–49
sausage:
    penne with ricotta and 84
    penne with sausage sauce 73
scallops, orecchiette with rocket and 57
shrimps:
    tagliatelle with brown shrimps
        and peas 58
silk handkerchiefs with green beans
    and pesto 92
spaghetti:
    from le Marche 62
    spaghetti, boiled tomato sauce with
        celery and carrots 37
    spaghetti in the bag 65
    with artichoke and parsley pesto 4
    with bottarga 71
    with clams and Prosecco 64
    with garlic, chilli, parsley and lemon 45
    with ginger and tomato 34
    with lemon 15
    with cherry tomatoes and two
        vinegars 7
    with marinated lobster 63
    with parsley and pancetta 83
    with pecorino 16
    with peppers, tomatoes and capers 35
    with plum tomatoes, capers and
        olives 5
    with prosciutto, peas and spring
        onions 87
    with roasted red mullet and olives 66
    with squid and zucchini 67
    with tomato purée 38
    with zucchini, capers and tomatoes 36
spinach: gnudi verdi 105
    rotolo stuffed with spinach 97
    spinach gnocchi 103
    spinach pasta 90
spirale with clams and prawns 53
squid, spaghetti with zucchini and 67
stuffed pasta 89–97

tagliatelle:
    tagliatelle alla carbonara with
        prosciutto 77
    with asparagus 22
    with brown shrimps and peas 58

with crème fraîche and rocket 19
with dried porcini and sage 42
with fresh figs and chilli 46
with fresh hazelnuts 8
with fresh walnuts 10
with girolle mushrooms 43
with gorgonzola 21
with green beans 11
with langoustines and ricotta 69
with lemon, cream and parsley 20
with mascarpone and fried
    breadcrumbs 18
with pancetta and borlotti 88
with prosciutto, rosemary and
    radicchio 78
taglierini:
    with clams and fried zucchini 70
    with fresh porcini 6
    with pancetta and trevise 85
    with quick tomato sauce 32
    with raw broad beans 12
    with red mullet and bay 68
    with slow-cooked tomato sauce 33
    with white truffles 9
tomatoes:
    gnocchi with tomato sauce 102
    orecchiette with fresh ricotta and 2
    pappardelle with pancetta, white wine,
        cream and 81
    pasta pieces with black olives and 91
    penne all'arrabbiata 25
    penne alla matriciana 74
    penne with aubergine, mozzarella
        and 26
    penne with balsamic vinegar 31
    penne with capers, ricotta salata and 1
    penne with dried porcini, cream and
        30
    penne with nutmeg and 27
    penne with sausage sauce 73
    rigatoni with beef, red wine and 76
    spaghetti, boiled tomato sauce with
        celery and carrots 37
    spaghetti from Le Marche 62
    spaghetti in the bag 65
    spaghetti with cherry tomatoes and
        two vinegars 7
    spaghetti with ginger and 34
    spaghetti with peppers, capers and 35
    spaghetti with plum tomatoes, capers
        and olives 5
    spaghetti with tomato purée 38
    spaghetti with zucchini, capers and 36

tagliatelle with green beans 11
taglierini with quick tomato sauce 32
taglerini with slow-cooked tomato
    sauce 33
trevise, taglierini with pancetta and 85
truffles: taglierini with white truffles 9

vegetarian sauces 23–49

walnuts, tagliatelle with 10

zucchini:
    farfalle with grilled aubergine and 47
    penne with deep-fried zucchini 48
    penne with mint and 28
    penne with mussels and 51
    penne with ricotta and 13
    spaghetti with capers, tomatoes
        and 36
    spaghetti with squid and 67
    taglierini with clams and fried
        zucchini 70

The authors would like to thank Tanya Nathan and Ronnie Bonnetti and all the staff at the River Cafe. Fiona MacIntyre, Imogen Fortes, Sarah Lavelle, David Loftus and Mark Porter.

1 3 5 7 9 10 8 6 4 2

Text © Rose Gray and Ruth Rogers 2006

First published in the United Kingdom in 2006 by Ebury Press, an imprint of Ebury Publishing, Random House UK Ltd., 20 Vauxhall Bridge Road, London SW1V 2SA

Random House Australia (Pty) Limited, 20 Alfred Street, Milsons Point, Sydney, New South Wales 2061, Australia

Random House New Zealand Limited, 18 Poland Road, Glenfield, Auckland 10, New Zealand

Random House (Pty) Limited, Isle of Houghton Corner of Boundary Road & Carse O'Gowrie Houghton, 2198, South Africa

Random House Publishers India Private Limited, 301 World Trade Tower, Hotel Intercontinental Grand Complex, Barakhamba Lane, New Delhi 110 001, India

Random House UK Limited Reg. No. 954009, www.randomhouse.co.uk

Papers used by Ebury Press are natural, recyclable products made from wood grown in sustainable forests.

A CIP catalogue record is available for this book from the British Library.

ISBN: 009191437X   ISBN: 9780091914370 (from Jan 2007)

Printed and bound in Italy by Graphicom SRL

Designed by Mark Porter Design, www.markporter.com

Copies are available at special rates for bulk orders. Contact the sales development team on 020 7840 8487 or visit www.booksforpromotions.co.uk for more information.